The Last Guide

L*The* Last Guide

A *Story of* Fish *and* Love

Ron Corbett

PENGUIN
VIKING

VIKING

Published by the Penguin Group

Penguin Books Canada Ltd, 10 Alcorn Avenue, Toronto, Ontario, Canada
M4V 3B2

Penguin Books Ltd, 80 Strand, London WC2R 0RL, England

Penguin Putnam Inc., 375 Hudson Street, New York, New York 10014, U.S.A.

Penguin Books Australia Ltd, Ringwood, Victoria, Australia

Penguin Books (NZ) Ltd, cnr Rosedale and Airborne Roads, Albany, Auckland
1310, New Zealand

Penguin Books Ltd, Registered Offices: Harmondsworth, Middlesex, England

First published 2001

1 2 3 4 5 6 7 8 9 10
Printed and bound in Canada on acid free paper ∞

National Library of Canada Cataloguing in Publication Data

Corbett, Ron, 1959–
The last guide : a story of fish and love

ISBN 0-670-91141-0

1. Fishing guides—Ontario—Algonquin Provincial Park.
2. Fishing guides. 3. Kuiack, Frank. 4. Fishing—Ontario—Algonquin Provincial
Park. 5. Fishing. I. Title.

SH572.O5C67 2001   799.1'2'09713147   C2001-902678-1

Visit Penguin Canada's website at **www.penguin.ca**

Contents

For my family:
Andrea, Dylan, Tara and Hailey.

Love of work
The blood singing in that
The fine, high rise of that into the work;
A man says: "I'm working"
Or: "I worked today"
Or: "I'm trying to make it work."

Raymond Carver

Prologue

I crested a hill on Highway 60 and saw the village of Whitney below me, a short strip of buildings bordering Galeairy Lake and the Madawaska River, a mile from the east gate of Algonquin Provincial Park. As I started down the hill I glanced at my watch: 6:30 P.M. I had an interview arranged for 7:00. I was going to be late.

I slowed down only slightly through the village— past the Toronto-Dominion Bank, the turnoff for the Foodmart and the Men Wah Tay gift shop, the Shell station, the Ontario Provincial Police detachment, then the buildings thinning out: a Stinson gas station, Opeongo Outfitters—foot heavy on the gas pedal once I cleared a boarded-up building that used to be the Howlin' Wolf restaurant. Twenty-eight minutes now to get to Arowhon Pines Resort, check in, drop off my bags and back out to meet a naturalist from the park who would be waiting at the turnoff for Pog Lake campground.

I was coming to Algonquin park to write a story on wolves—recent DNA testing seemed to show that the wolves in Algonquin park were not timber wolves, as long assumed, but red wolves, a species once thought virtually extinct, except for a single pack located on the Texas-Louisiana border. The U.S. Fish & Wildlife Service had spent tens of millions of dollars protecting that pack, moving it to a fenced wildlife preserve, allowing it to breed. Now it looked like there were thousands of the animals right here in north-central Ontario. Man is foolish and ignorant; wolves laugh themselves silly.

It is in August that naturalists at the park hold public wolf howls: every Thursday night hundreds of tourists line up on Highway 60 in the dead of night while naturalists imitate the howl of wolves, in the hopes that a pack they located earlier in the week will howl back. I was driving through Whitney on August 1. Mike Runtz, the naturalist who has written a book on wolves in the park, *The Howls of August*, would be waiting for me—twenty-three minutes from now—to try and find a wolf pack that night. I drove a little faster, wondering how long a naturalist would wait for a reporter he'd never met. A politician—depending on the politician, level of government and personal need for attention—you could count on for as long as an hour. A naturalist, I had no way of knowing.

Then I saw the turnoff for Arowhon, braked quickly

Red wolf

and turned right. The resort is not off the highway, but somewhere down a gravel road. I drove through the shadows and glare of a sun setting behind pine and hardwood trees, much too fast on a road I'd never driven before, fishtailing on curves and wondering how far I'd have to go.

It's not a complicated procedure, trying to find a pack of wolves in Algonquin park. You simply go out in the evening, howl like a wolf and hope a wolf howls back. Go with a partner so you can try group howls. Try it three times and, if nothing happens, move on.

3

Tourists on Highway 60, on their way to a wolf howl

Runtz was not upset when I arrived forty minutes late. That night we howled by mist-enshrouded lakes and dried-up creek beds; on granite outcrops where we could see headlights moving down Highway 60; and in trailhead parking lots that seemed to close in on us. The sky had cleared, after two days of torrential rain, and we howled with mist swirling around our feet and the tops of spruce trees silhouetted against an indigo sky splashed with stars. It was one of those picture-perfect Algonquin Highland evenings, right down to the crescent moon suspended above the trees. The howl of a wolf would have made it complete, but after three hours of driving and howling, we had yet to hear one. The creeks and streams that surrounded us were running

4

high because of the recent rainstorm, and we heard running water all night. There was a strong wind as well.

"The perfect night for a wolf howl is clear, no wind, with just a slight chill in the air," Runtz said. "Sound travels a long way on a night like that. Tonight, with all this water and wind I can barely hear my own howls."

We stayed out until nearly midnight, travelling up and down Highway 60, howling at the stars and the silhouetted trees, but the only animal to answer us was a barred owl. Eventually I made my way back to Arowhon. We would try again tomorrow night. If we didn't locate a wolf pack, the first public wolf howl of the season would have to be cancelled.

I asked Runtz how often that's happened, cancelling a wolf howl.

He shrugged.

"It happens," he said. "Not all that often, but it happens."

I spent a restless night thinking of ways to write a story about an animal I'll never see or, possibly, hear.

The next night I was back on Highway 60, on the west side of Algonquin park, where another two-person wolf search crew had been working the night before. I howled by Canoe Lake, where painter Tom Thomson drowned in 1917, and by the Oxtongue River, the Tea Lake campground and Cache Lake, where the majestic Highland Inn once stood. The wind was stronger than the previous night and the runoff on the creeks and rivers seemed to have increased. That night we didn't even hear a barred owl.

The public wolf howl was cancelled.

I spent the morning at Arowhon, typing notes on my computer and wondering what to do next. I had interviewed naturalists; corresponded with the McMaster University professor who had co-authored the DNA study; the facts had been gathered—I was just missing the tourists, and the wolves.

"Push back the story," my editor said. "We still have three more weeks for them to find a wolf pack. As soon as they hold a wolf call, we'll go back and finish the story."

A good plan, but it left an empty day ahead of me. I sat on the verandah of the dining lodge at Arowhon, drinking coffee and looking at the canoes travelling across Little Joe Lake, wondering what to do that afternoon. Finally, I decided to drive to Whitney. The day before I had noticed a stuffed wolf head on display in the Men Wah Tay gift shop, a sight that would outrage everyone I've interviewed so far. Maybe someone in Whitney had a different take on the wolves.

I parked my car at the Shell station and went to the side door, where I'd noticed a group of men sitting the day before. There were chairs and milk crates set up outside; in the back of the garage was another door, which connected to the Algonquin Lunchbar, one of three restaurants in Whitney and as likely a local gathering spot as any I'd seen.

I walked up to a middle-aged man sitting on a milk crate, fanning himself with a newspaper. I tried to think of something clever to say, couldn't.

"Hot enough for you?"

"Going to be hotter tomorrow," he replied.

"You've heard the weather forecast?" I asked. I would be driving back to Ottawa the following day, and my air conditioning had been acting up.

"No."

I nodded. "I wonder if you can help me," I said then, and identified myself, explained what I was doing in Algonquin park and gave a brief synopsis of the red-wolf/timber-wolf debate.

"They're timber wolves," he said. "I've never seen any red wolves, so I don't know what they look like. But the wolves in the park, they're timber wolves."

Good. Very good.

"What's your name?" I asked.

"Don't want to tell you."

"Sorry?"

"Don't want to tell you my name. Don't want to be quoted in the newspaper. Just get in trouble that way."

I argued a little—what trouble could there possibly be? It's a story about wolves—but he was adamant.

"All right," I said. "Is there anyone in town who might talk to me? I'd like to speak to someone who lives outside the park. I've done nothing but interview naturalists and scientists since I've been here."

He thought for a moment, sitting there on the milk crate sunning himself. Finally he said, "You should go see Frank Kuiack. He's one of the councillors in town. Knows all about wolves. Could even have one as a pet in his backyard for all I know."

I looked up Kuiack's name (it's pronounced Kweeack) in a telephone book by the pay phone at the end of the lunch counter. I called and after several rings, just as I was about to hang up, a man's voice came on the line.

"Hello."

"Hello. Is this Frank Kuiack?"

"Right on."

I smiled at that. Couldn't remember the last time I had heard that phrase. I identified myself and told Kuiack someone at the Shell station thought he might be able to help with a story I was working on.

"What's the story?" he asked.

"It's about the wolves in the park. I'm told you know a fair bit about wolves."

"What do you want to know?"

"Well, I'd prefer not to do this over the phone. Is there any chance we could meet?"

"Come on over."

"Now?"

"I'm here now."

I found Kuiack's house after driving by it twice, the building hidden behind a tall cedar hedge. I pulled into a driveway and parked behind a silver Dodge Dakota pickup. I looked around, and even then, that first day, it seemed as if I had left one world and entered another.

The yard around the house was littered with boats: old Chestnut canoes; aluminum rowboats; big, burnished brown Peterboroughs. I counted fourteen— leaning against a workshop, lying beside a vegetable garden, stacked behind a woodpile. Some looked long unused and were shrouded in green plastic tarps, like body bags.

The house itself had metal, fire-escape stairs leading to a screen door on the second floor. There was another door, which seemed to lead into a basement; which one was the main door I couldn't tell. The house seemed to have a basement and a second floor, but no ground level. I walked around the house, looking for another door, but couldn't find one.

"You want the door in front of you. Come up the stairs."

I looked up at the windows but couldn't see anyone.

I walked through the doorway leading into the basement. Inside, the room was dark, but gradually I saw stairs in front of me. Walking up I passed fishing rods and Folgers coffee cans, snowshoes and fishing-tackle boxes, muddy hip waders and rain jackets. When I reached the top—the house was built on a small rise,

9

giving the illusion of no main floor—I walked into a large, brightly lit space.

The room was a combination kitchen and living room, although it wasn't appliances or furniture that I noticed first, but stuffed fish. They seemed to be everywhere—on the walls, perched on the television. All trout, either speckled or lake trout. There were stuffed mammals as well—a badger, an otter, a fox—staring out at me from stairs leading to an attic, from the top of the fridge, from wooden shelves.

In the middle of the room was a kitchen table and toward the far end a couch, a coffee table and two wooden chairs in front of a south-facing window. On the wall above the couch was a metal sign: *Thank You For Not Smoking.*

On the couch below was a short man dressed in green work clothes, Buckmasters ball cap and work boots. He was smiling and smoking a cigarette.

"Mr. Kuiack?"

"Right on. You the reporter?"

"That's right." I tried hard to suppress a smile but Kuiack caught it.

"Tried to quit once. It didn't take."

It's never a good idea to start an interview by making someone defensive, but I had to ask.

"Why keep the sign then?"

"Perfectly good sign," he said.

I nodded.

"Would you like a coffee?"

"Love one." I pulled out a chair from the kitchen table, sat down and quickly ran through the story as the coffee brewed: red wolves, timber wolves, DNA, the U.S. Fish & Wildlife Service, tens of millions of dollars, naturalists, scientists.

What did he think?

"Well, there is something different about the wolves in the park," he said. "I was up North a long time ago, seen the timber wolves up there, and they look different from what we've got. Up there they're darker, and bigger. Maybe what we have are red wolves."

"The scientists seem to think so."

"They may be right. It happens from time to time."

Kuiack brought me a cup of coffee and I asked some more questions about wolves. He said he'd seen them a few times when he was in the bush in Algonquin park—not all that often, wolves don't like to be seen, but he'd seen them a few times all right. Once, he'd seen a wolf chase a deer right into a lake, the deer swimming around trying to get away, the wolf tracking it on the shore, right there every time the deer tried to get out of the water, trapped like no animal he'd ever seen before. He watched it for more than two hours and would have loved to have seen how it all played out, but he had to make camp before nightfall, so he left.

Another time he'd seen an entire wolf pack moving

through a burn. It was early autumn. He'd never seen anything like that since.

"We were fishing on Pen Lake," he said. "Had a party with me."

"A party? You were a fishing guide?"

"That's right."

"How long did you do that for?" I asked, taking a sip of coffee.

It was intended as nothing more than conversation between serious questions and note-taking about wolves. Thirty minutes to go and I would be back on the road, a productive afternoon.

"I still guide."

"I didn't think anyone still guided in the park."

"You're right," he said. "They're pretty much all gone. I may be the last one."

Seven weeks later the story on the wolves appeared in the *Ottawa Citizen*'s weekly magazine. For the first time in nearly twenty years, the wolf howl was cancelled every week until the final Thursday in August. When the public howl was finally held—more than eight hundred people showed up, some from as far away as Pittsburgh —no wolves were heard.

The following week, the paper ran a much longer story on Frank Kuiack. He was, indeed, the last of the old-time fishing guides still working full-time in Algonquin park.

Photo by Julie Oliver

In the months that followed my first meeting with Kuiack I would come to know the names and stories of many of those guides: Joe Lavally, Basil Sawyer, Sam Beaver, the Luckasavitch brothers and Tom Thomson, who was working as a fishing guide at Mowat Lodge the summer he drowned in Canoe Lake.

The stories, like the park itself, were beautiful, moving, sometimes comic, sometimes tragic, but always carrying a resonance of other stories. Much like the story of Frank Kuiack himself.

Kuiack's life seemed to be a counterpoint to the many changes that had taken place over the years, not only around Algonquin park, but elsewhere in Canada.

While all these changes led to the slow disappearance of the fishing guides in the Algonquin Highlands, Kuiack never abandoned the calling. Today he is the last practitioner of a business, a trade, an *art*, that will die with him.

Kuiack didn't change after the *Citizen* story was published, nor in my months of researching and writing this book, but I did. I continue to marvel at the happenstance beginnings of the journey about to come. If those wolves had shown up, I would never have met Kuiack. I would have returned to Ottawa, written up the wolves, and gone on to something else, never knowing what I had missed.

As it was, meeting Kuiack might have led to nothing more than an extended passage in the wolf story, or a short profile some day when I would be sitting back in Ottawa, looking for a story idea.

Instead, when I finished my interview that first day and was about to leave, I put my coffee cup in the sink and made my way down the stairs. Frank had gone outside ahead of me.

In the basement I spotted a room I hadn't noticed before. It was tucked away in a far corner, almost hidden behind a half-finished partition wall. I took a quick look and saw it was a bedroom. Clothes were strewn on the floor, a long rectangular table was covered with fishing lures—spoons, spinners, jigs—and on the bed was a small pillow and sleeping bag. I saw several wall calendars from sporting goods stores, a framed picture I would learn later was Kuiack's father—and there, stapled to a back door, where he could see it as he lay in bed, was a map of the canoe routes of Algonquin park.

It was the bedroom of a boy.

"Frank," I heard myself saying, when we were standing by my car. "Why don't we go fishing one of these days."

Frank

Frank was born in 1935, the year the first automobiles reached Algonquin Provincial Park on Highway 60, a new road constructed as a Depression-era make-work project. He was raised on a farm on Long Lake, Ontario, a mile from the east gate of Algonquin park.

At the entrance to Mud Bay, the St. Anthony Lumber Company used to stack slabs of bark stripped from giant pine, so everyone called the cluster of small farms and cabins around the Kuiacks' "Slab Town." The cabins along the Madawaska River, near Long Lake, were called Jerusalem. Paradise was the name given to the homes built on Hay Creek, on a northeast hill overlooking a sawmill.

The nearest town was Whitney, on the eastern shore of Long Lake, where it emptied into the Madawaska River. It consisted of the sawmill, a trading post, a Canadian National Railways depot, a post office in the home of Ned Cannon, a Department of Lands and Forests office, Dr. Post's house, an Anglican and a Catholic church, an Anglican and a Catholic school, and half a dozen lumber company bunkhouses.

Frank's father, for whom he was named, had sixteen children; Frank was his youngest son. Frank Sr. worked as a foreman for the McRae Lumber Company at a sawmill on Lake of Two Rivers. He was born in Wilno, Canada's oldest Polish settlement, the son of a Polish couple who had emigrated from Koziki two years before he was born.

Like most people in Slab Town, the Kuiack family didn't own a car or a horse. To reach Whitney they could walk around the lake, following the railway line, or they could row a boat across Long Lake. Frank's earliest memory is of being in a boat with his parents as they rowed to town.

When he was four, Frank caught his first trout, using a steel line and a curled nail he had sharpened with a file and baited with a whitefish tail. It was a large lake trout, and he pulled it into the boat hand over hand. From then on, he fished whenever he could. He learned where Long Lake dropped to depths of 120 feet or more, and where it rose in stony shoals. He learned where fish went to spawn in the fall, where they swam in schools in the spring and what bait worked best in each season.

Frank's family owned only one pair of "school clothes," a good pair of boy's trousers and shoes, so only

Whitney, Ontario, in the 1930s

one boy could attend school at a time. Before one could enter school, the next-eldest brother had to graduate. On days when he was fishing, Frank hoped Edmund would stay in school forever.

Before long, strangers joined him on the lake to fish. The strangers had pale skin and uncallused hands, and they didn't speak like the men he knew. There was a singsong quality to their voices—the vowels drawn out and inflected—a leisurely way of speaking unlike the clipped, harsh talk of his neighbours. His father explained that the strangers came from a place called "the States."

One day in late spring, when Frank was eight, he rowed to town to run errands. Along the way he caught two lake trout. As he pulled the boat ashore below Dr. Post's house two strangers stood watching him.

"Son, come here. We want to talk with you a minute."

Frank turned, looked at the men and wondered, briefly, what he had done wrong. When he reached them one said, "You caught some nice fish there. You seem to know the lake fairly well."

It sounded like a question, but Frank wasn't sure. He pointed across the lake to his home.

"I live just over there, sir."

The two men looked to where he was pointing and nodded.

"Son, do you think you could take us fishing? Row us around the lake for an hour or two and show us where the good spots are?"

He thought it a strange question. He had to fetch the mail at Cannon's, then help his father split a fallen white pine that had been struck by lightning not far from their home. Enough wood to last a year. This was no time to go fishing.

He started to refuse but saw, when he looked up, that the stranger was holding something in his hand—paper money, folded in half and thicker than a store catalogue. More money than Frank had seen in his life.

The stranger smiled.

"We'll pay you."

Frank told the two strangers he could spare two hours. They caught twenty-three fish.

To Frank's surprise, the men had no interest in trout: they were after smallmouth bass, a species that had been introduced to Long Lake by the Department of Lands and Forests before he was born. He rowed the boat to a small bay where deadheads and water lilies extended far into the water, and motioned for the men to start fishing. The men had steel poles and wooden plugs and the fishing line made a loud, metallic sound, like cable uncoiling from a drum, when the plugs were cast. A fish was caught with virtually every cast. Frank had never seen men as giddy and childish as the two strangers, laughing and clinking their silver flasks as he netted their fish. Hell, it was only bass.

Bass gave a better fight than trout, and they tasted all right, but Frank found them ugly. Nothing like a speckled trout, the way the colours on a speckled's sides changed the bigger it got so you could tell, by the graduations of amber and yellow, how old it was, a mature speckled trout as burnished and beautiful as well-oiled mahogany—that was a beautiful fish. Plus, and maybe there was something proprietary about this, but it was the nature of things, bass weren't from around here. They were interlopers and you had to acknowledge that. Trout were beautiful and bass were ugly and now bass were everywhere. It made you wonder.

But it was bass the men wanted. So Frank rowed

back and forth across the small bay, stopping only to net the fish, as the men got happier and drunker. That afternoon, when he pulled the boat ashore in front of the circle of white canvas tents and the dark-coloured automobiles below the sawmill, the two men kept slapping him on the back and congratulating him.

Later, he showed his father the five dollars he had been paid for two hours' work—more money than his father earned for a full shift at McRae's. Frank was told to give the money to his mother.

The next day Frank rowed back to the circle of tents. It was a sunny day so he unbuttoned his shirt and lay with his back against the rock. After a few minutes he got up, moved a small metal pail filled with frogs into the shade and went back to waiting.

That day, Frank made another five dollars. The following day, four.

"Frankie, it is good you make this money," his father told him that night. "It makes your mother happy."

Frank nodded. His father seemed happy as well.

"You goin' to become a fishing guide, eh? To Algonquin park you go next?"

"I don't need to go to the park. I can catch bass right here. Trout too, if the Americans had the sense."

"No, don't teach them how to catch trout, Frank," said his father. "They see that fish, they never leave. Have to live with those men all year long."

"Don't worry. It's just bass they want."

His father ran his hand through his son's hair.

"A fishin' guide, eh? We'll need you in the bush one day, Frank. It's good now, though, the money those men give you. It's good."

His father was unsteady on his feet, rocking gently back and forth, his arm resting on Frank's shoulder as they watched the sun setting behind the hills over Long Lake. The way the sun hit the white pine made the trees look on fire.

"It's good," he said, one more time.

Few of the fishing guides around Whitney—the men with licences that allowed them to work in Algonquin park—made money from bass. They guided for speckled or lake trout, many of them on Opeongo, the biggest lake in the park, virtually a landlocked sea, where you could catch record-setting lakers.

So they were intrigued with this scrawny Polish kid who was making a man's wages catching bass on Long Lake. Local guides—Basil Sawyer; A. C. Parks; the Luckasavitch brothers, Alex, Jack, Felix and Paul— would see the boy beach his rowboat, not even a canoe, by the tent city, would see a string of fish being unloaded and men climbing out of the boat unsteadily.

"Frankie, how much do those men pay you?" asked Sawyer one day.

"Four dollars a day."

"Do they feed you?"

"No."

Sawyer shook his head.

"Should feed you. Don't make it hard for the real men, eh, boy? Guiding without being fed—it's not done that way."

After that Frank thought of demanding lunch, but never dared. He did not want to anger the men; and, besides, when you came right down to it, he was never all that hungry. He did start to avoid the other guides when he saw them in Whitney, though, and kept quiet about how much money he was making.

Frank rowed his boat to the tent city every morning that summer of 1942 after finishing his chores, and the men came to know him by name.

"Francis, you're late today," said Dr. McKenzie, a dentist from Akron, Ohio, one day. It was early August, and the promise of heat was already thick in the air. Frank motioned to a nearby hill and explained that a cow had gone off, after being let out to graze, and he had had to chase it home.

"Well, it's not cows we're after this morning, Francis, it's fish," said Dr. McKenzie. "So it's a good thing you've come. We have no interest in catching cows, none whatsoever, although I'm sure you're quite good at that as well. You've brought the bait, have you?"

Frank held up the pail of frogs.

"Very good. And your boat, we shall take it for our party. Doctors Archibald and Stewart will take mine."

Frank waved to two men standing by the shore, one thin, one portly, dressed in nearly identical tweed knickers and fishing vests.

"Very good. Well, if it's all settled, let's get going. Francis, perhaps you could give some frogs to our friends, so we're not passing them around out on the lake."

Dr. McKenzie liked to organize things. Frank got another pail from his boat, took some cheesecloth from his pocket, covered the second pail, and gave it to the doctors, who nodded politely.

"Now then. To the fish I say. They are out there right now, no doubt wondering why we have been tardy in visiting them this morning. A cow is the reason we shall give them when we meet."

Frank began to row. Dr. McKenzie opened a silver flask, took a long sip and looked around.

"A most lovely morning, Francis. Most lovely, indeed. You are blessed to live here. You likely don't realize that, but it is the God's truth. You are blessed."

Frank nodded.

"I would live in my tent all year if I could. But teeth and money, they have become the cornerstones of my life—a strange life you might say, as might our fishing partners, but teeth and money are our lives now. Would it surprise you if I said I did not give a damn about another man's teeth?"

Frank shook his head.

"Of course not. What sane man would care? It is an oddity, Francis, how a modern man makes his money."

They rowed to a small bay on the far side of the lake, Dr. McKenzie talking about teeth and drinking steadily, Frank looking at the shadows on the lake and calculating the best place to start casting. When he had decided he stopped rowing and motioned for the dentist to start fishing.

"So this is where we shall do battle today, Francis? Very well, let us begin."

The other dentists pulled up alongside, then rowed several feet away. None of the men could cast with accuracy, and only the portly one, Dr. Stewart, had any sense of how big the fish at the end of his line was. Dr. McKenzie lost three plugs and a leader by reeling in too quickly. Still, they managed to catch a dozen smallmouth bass.

They returned to the tent city for lunch, Frank waiting by the shore, and then headed out again, the dentists by now thoroughly drunk. "To battle," yelled Dr. McKenzie, as Frank pushed the boat offshore. The other dentists raised their silver flasks: "To battle."

They fished for another two hours, with drunken toasts and loud shouts across the lake. Once, Dr. McKenzie nearly tipped the boat when he leaned over to see how big the bass was that Frank was netting—Frank jumped to the other side of the boat just in time, but the dentist didn't seem to notice.

Then, late in the afternoon and nearly time for Frank to return home, Dr. McKenzie gave his longest sermon of the day: "Is it right," he began, "that a grown man should make his money from teeth, Francis? You, a boy, are more a man than any doctor of dentistry science, and you should never forget it. As a species, I think man should be liberated from the tyranny of teeth, from the care and upkeep of teeth, from the needless enrichment of men such as myself, whose only skill is knowing more about teeth than most men.

"What even is the need for teeth? Can we not grind our food? Can we not use blenders, many kinds of which are now readily available? Has modern science not shown us the way? Look here, Francis, look at how easy it would be." And with that Dr. McKenzie pulled his teeth from his mouth, a full upper and lower plate.

"Aff simfle aff phab," he said, and threw the teeth across the lake. They landed not far from a wooden plug. The dentist raised his arms in the air, like a runner crossing the finish line. He stood up and rocked the boat, yelling "Freeephum. Freeephum!" and he was still shouting like that when a large bass surfaced, grabbed the teeth and disappeared.

Dr. McKenzie lowered his arms and stopped rocking the boat. He looked at the spreading circle of ripples, at the centre of which had once been his teeth.

"Bloony fish jusb fook my feeph."

Frank shook his head no. Fish didn't eat teeth.

"How phan you say phaf, Franphis? You jusb saw iph."

For a long time they looked at the spot where the bass had surfaced, waiting for the teeth to float up. In that time Dr. McKenzie seemed to sober. Eventually, he sat down and held his head in his hands while Frank rowed, looking for the teeth, refusing to believe a fish had swallowed them, thinking they must have come up near some water lilies, hidden from view; but he never found them.

That night, Dr. McKenzie packed up and headed back to Akron. Doctors Stewart and Archibald stayed one more day, continuing the search for the missing teeth, but without success. When his father asked him that night how the fishing had gone, Frank told him in Polish that they had caught many bass, but Dr. McKenzie had lost his teeth to a fish they never caught. Hard to judge a day like that.

His father asked how the dentist had lost his teeth to a fish and Frank said the man had thrown them into the lake, but couldn't explain why. Frank understood fish pretty well, and was beginning to understand money, but drinking, yearning, teeth—all that was a mystery.

"So there's a bass out there in the lake with a good pair of American-made false teeth?" asked his father.

Frank thought so.

"Ever catch that fish, Frank, you bring it to me. I need some teeth."

When the soft maples started to turn that year, in early September, Frank continued to row across Long Lake, but the number of white canvas tents below the sawmill was dwindling. Soon there were fewer than a dozen, by late September only two, then finally one, inhabited by an old merchant seaman from Boston who never hired Frank.

For the first time in his life Frank found himself wanting something he could not have, the feeling lingering long enough to become a yearning, and it was that new wet blanket of an emotion that descended upon him in the autumn of 1942.

Frank did his chores and noticed the sere colours of autumn around him, but with little interest. As he chopped wood he wondered what was disturbing his sleep, causing that awkward hesitation in just about everything he did. He talked to his brother Edmund, with whom he shared a bed—all of the Kuiack children shared beds, the boys in one bedroom, the girls in another—but Edmund was no help. Looking for the words to describe what he was feeling, Frank, all of eight years old, had said he was "lonely," although he didn't think that was right, just the best he could do. His brother had laughed.

"How can you feel lonely in this house?"

"I don't know. I can't explain it."

"You miss the money, Frank, that's all."

"Mother still has some of the money. All I have to do

is ask if I want anything in town. I don't think it's the
money."

Edmund shook his head and stifled a yawn.

"Maybe you miss the fishing."

Frank nodded and said, "Maybe that's it," although he
didn't think so. He had been fishing for as long as he
could remember, but this feeling was new. It had something to do with fish, when you stopped to think it
through, but there was more: the look in a man's eyes
when he landed the biggest fish he had ever caught, the
moment sometimes so uncomfortably intimate that
Frank had to look away; or the way paper money felt in
his pocket, his fingers rubbing the bills until they turned
soft and downy; or Long Lake early in the morning, with
mist rising and Frank rowing his boat to the tent city,
anticipating the day. It was all of that, and yet there was
something more as well. He struggled to sleep that night,
feeling for the first time a dread of the seasons changing.

The snows came late that year. Come spring the rivers in
the highlands were low and sluggish, something Frank
had never seen before. He had worried about the
fishing, but caught the biggest lake trout of his life,
twenty-one pounds, the first week of May. Shortly afterwards, the first canvas tent reappeared.

That year, 1943, he sold wood to the fishermen, and
some of his father's moonshine, a commodity prized at
least as much as the wood and guiding services: the near-

est liquor store was in Barry's Bay, fifty kilometres away.

In mid-July Dr. McKenzie returned, and Frank was glad to see him. Two days earlier he had taken out a party from Columbus, Ohio, and they had nearly filled the rowboats with bass. The next day, though, his three fishermen caught fewer than ten fish between them. Some of the fish were fine—one was over six pounds—but the men had seen the boatload of fish caught the previous day, and it seemed to Frank they had paid their four dollars grudgingly.

That night he dreamed that the men talked about him around their campfire, saying unkind things. When Frank saw Dr. McKenzie he seemed a long-lost friend.

"Francis, how good to see you again," said the dentist. "Did you ever manage to find my teeth?"

Dr. McKenzie sat in front of his tent, beside a campfire, where a skillet of bacon was frying, a percolator of coffee to the side of the grill. Frank shook his head.

"Well, I must say I felt like quite a donkey's ass for some time after that little incident. Doctors Archibald and Stewart have certainly enjoyed the retelling of the story, although I must agree it's not a bad yarn, as stories about teeth go. Tell me, Francis, do you think a fish really swallowed them?"

Frank shrugged.

"We shall never know then. A mystery. You're absolutely right. We should be grateful. There are so few mysteries about teeth."

Frank sat on a rock and let the dentist talk.

"You have brought firewood this year, Francis. That's yours, down by the shore, is it not?"

Dr. McKenzie pointed with a walking stick to a stacked pyramid of maple and birch logs by the water. Frank nodded.

"Yes, I was told there was firewood for sale, when I arrived last night. They said a Polish boy, short and not speaking much English, was selling it at a reasonable rate. I thought it must have been you. A new sideline, Francis? We don't pay enough for the bass?"

"Pay fine," said Frank, momentarily worried. "Wood not fish."

"Yes, of course. Wood not fish. You're quite right. And why shouldn't you make money from trees. Everyone else around here does, right? Why not, Francis. This is a good service you offer. I will avail myself of it later tonight."

Dr. McKenzie put down his cup of coffee, leaned over the grill, and said, "Now, Francis, where shall we fish today?"

Frank rowed across the lake, not far from his home. It was where he had gone fishing with the party from Columbus.

"We don't normally go this far, Francis," said the dentist. "This is a favourite spot, is it?"

Frank nodded his head.

"Very well then."

Frank rowed to an inlet on Mud Bay, pointed with his finger to some water lilies, and Dr. McKenzie began to fish. On his first cast the dentist hooked a bass, the rod bowing and jerking over the water as he reeled in. It was a nice fish, nearly five pounds, and Frank was pleased. He rowed back and forth across the inlet for the rest of the morning, and Dr. McKenzie caught fish with virtually every cast. At this rate, thought Frank, they might outfish the party from Columbus. With just one rod.

In mid-afternoon, when it was just about time to row back to the tent city, the treble-hooked wooden plug arced once more above the water. Frank had stopped rowing and sat, his chin resting on his hands, the net on his knees. It was a hot day and he had taken off his shirt. On that cast it seemed as if the bass took the plug before it even hit the water. Frank straightened his body. The fish was huge.

The fishing line went off the reel in such a rush that it sounded like the buzz of a mosquito. Frank had never seen line go out that fast. The fish was making its way to a stand of deadheads and Frank pointed excitedly.

"Yes, Francis, I see it. I could well lose him if he comes up there, although I really have no choice in the matter. I can't stop him. Did you see him? How big do you think he is?"

Frank didn't bother answering. His attention was on

the line going out and the deadheads one hundred yards away. If the fish went under those deadheads and jumped there would be no way of catching him. The line would tangle and the fish would pull free for sure.

But the fish dove, and that was its mistake. When the line went slack Dr. McKenzie reeled in quickly, then played the fish away from the deadheads. He had improved since last year, Frank noticed, and wondered where else he fished. When the fish had been played clear of the submerged trees it jumped, but it was too late. Forty-five minutes later the fish was brought beside the boat, too tired to fight. It was the biggest bass Frank had ever seen.

"Francis," said Dr. McKenzie, breathing heavily and wiping his brow after the fish was safely in the boat. "What a wonderful, glorious, beat-the-band bass we have just caught. My goodness, son, we shall have that fish stuffed and hung on my study wall."

That night Frank slept soundly.

The fishing for the rest of July was the best Frank had ever seen on Long Lake, although by August it slowed, as it did at the end of every summer, when the bass were well fed and lazy, and many weeks had passed since they spawned—that brief time of the year when they were hungry for neither food nor sex, content with life and hard to hunt. In August Frank had to work extra hard for his money, moving the boat several times, trying a combination of bait, casting, trolling and jigging before he finally found fish. On those days, after some stranger had fished for as long as a week without so much as a bite, he would be cheerfully slapped on the back until it hurt.

It was, in many ways, his favourite time of the year, but it was on just one such hot August day that he discovered his guiding days were over.

There were no warning signs. He pulled the rowboat up on shore, took out the pail of frogs and his fishing net and made his way home. He passed the barns—one for the pigs, one for the cows—and the woodshed where he would collect wood for the evening meal as soon as he had dropped off his fishing equipment. He looked quickly at the vegetable garden, to see if the second planting of potatoes had started flowering, then placed the pail of frogs under the porch and went into the house.

He cut through the kitchen and made his way up the back stairs to the boys' bedroom. He wanted to put his four dollars in his room until he could give it to his mother. Once, when he had started chopping wood after guiding, he had left the money in his pocket. Sweat had moistened the bills and they had torn in his pocket. When he gave the tattered pieces of paper to his mother he felt like crying.

But that day on the bed he shared with Edmund he found a pair of crisply ironed grey pants and freshly polished black shoes.

His mother stuck her head in the room. "Edmund will be working in the camps this winter with your father, Francis."

Frank was going to school.

Fishing
PART I

When I asked Frank Kuiack if we could go fishing he agreed, but said he couldn't go until September. He was booked until then. So it was Labour Day Monday when I returned to Whitney.

I used the intervening time to read up on Algonquin park, looking for clues as to why Frank Kuiack was the last guide. I went way back and learned the Algonquin Highlands stand on the southernmost fringes of the Canadian Shield, formed by the advance and retreat of four continental glaciers over almost a million years. The movement of ice left behind granite and gneiss; shallow, infertile soil; a patchwork of deciduous and coniferous forests; the headwaters of five major rivers—the Madawaska, Petawawa, Oxtongue, L'Amable du Fond and Bonnechere—and thousands of lakes.

For millennia, paleo-Indians moved through the highlands between the Great Lakes to the west and the Ottawa River to the east. They were followed by woodland Indians such as the Ojibwa and the Algonquin, who used this vast height of land primarily to hunt and fish. By the mid-eighteenth century French fur traders travelled regularly along the Ottawa River, but only a few ventured to the highlands to the southwest.

There was simply no reason to come. The land was inhospitable to farming, and was of no strategic military or political value. It was only the demand for squared timber by the Royal Navy that finally brought the lumber companies to the area in the mid-nineteenth century. (The Opeongo Settlement Road, intended to run from Renfrew County to Opeongo Lake, stopped at the foot of the highlands, as if it had suddenly dawned on the settlers: "Why bother?")

All three of Canada's oceans had been discovered and mapped before any European explored the Algonquin Highlands. The land simply did not allow for the grand acts of civilization—the building of cities, the growing of food, the creating of commerce—so civilization stayed away.

Algonquin park was even created by a government bureaucrat who had never been to the area. Alexander Kirkwood, a clerk with the Ontario Department of Crown Lands, suggested a provincial park for the area in 1885, the year the last spike was driven in the Canadian

Pacific Railway. Kirkwood was convinced the government's plans for settling what was called the Ottawa-Huron Tract were unworkable, and eight years later Algonquin Provincial Park was established by an act of the Ontario legislature.

It was an easy decision—no one wanted to live here anyway. The highlands were a place for people passing through, on their way to somewhere else, a place for nomads and dreamers. Perhaps if you travelled far enough in the right direction, over the next forested hill, across the next lake, you might disappear forever. Over the years many people seemed to have tried exactly that, from Tom Thomson to E. B. White.

And yet, after the park was established it wasn't long before a steady stream of visitors started coming to the highlands. For there was one last historical and geographical oddity to the area.

As the last of the glaciers retreated from the highlands eleven thousand years ago, cold-water fish followed, leaving warm-water fish such as pike, muskellunge and bass to die in the meltwater. Land barriers later prevented their migration into the park.

After the last glacier was gone, trapped in the more than 1,500 lakes of Algonquin park were cold-water trout. Lots and lots of cold-water trout.

Trout belong to the Salmonidae family, which has three distinct genera, nearly two dozen species and an almost

George Hayes fishing party, on Rain Lake, 1896

Courtesy of Algonquin Park Museum

infinite number of subspecies and hybrids. Every fish in the family, from rainbow trout to chinook salmon, is considered a game fish, some being the most sought after in the world. The trout caught in Algonquin park—lake trout and brook trout—are the same species as bull trout, Dolly Varden and Arctic char.

Brook, or speckled trout, are dark brown to gold, with wavy lines on their backs, square or slightly forked tails and small pinkish spots surrounded by blue halos on their sides. Such trout have been known to reach fifteen pounds, although anything above two pounds is considered a fine catch.

Lake trout, which have exceeded one hundred pounds when caught in nets, are the second-largest fish in the Salmonidae family. Only the chinook, or king salmon, is larger. It's a fast swimmer and an aggressive predator, with a slender, torpedo-shaped body, a deeply forked tail and mottled, white spots on dark-brown colouring. Lake trout are found in only two thousand lakes in Ontario. One hundred and fifty of those lakes are in Algonquin park.

The first trip by a sports fisherman to the Algonquin Highlands might have taken place in the early 1880s. George Hayes from Buffalo, New York, was a wealthy industrialist and an avid trout fisherman. He arranged transportation with various lumber companies and hired Indian guides in Huntsville to show him the "good spots." He was so impressed with the fishing he returned every year.

Before long other wealthy fishermen started coming to the highlands, using the lumber-company tote roads to get their canoes and gear into the lakes. After it opened in 1896, the fishermen used the Ottawa, Arnprior and Parry Sound Railway as well. In 1908, however, the steady trickle of sports fishermen became a torrent. In that year the first two hotels in Algonquin park opened for business.

The Hotel Algonquin, on Joe Lake, was built by Tom Merrill of Rochester, New York. It was open six months of the year, and was a decidedly rustic-looking retreat, with cedar siding still covered in bark. It was a popular base for fishing parties right from the start, partly because of its superb meals and also because of its location next to the railway station at Joe Lake.

And then there was the Highland Inn. Built by the Grand Trunk Railway at Cache Lake, the Highland Inn was one of the most luxurious resorts in Ontario. Open year-round, the inn started with ten rooms, but soon added two wings to meet the demand. Even so, for many years the inn erected tents to house its overflow guests. At the Highland Inn there were tennis courts, a band-shell, boathouses and a store. Even the picnic lunches (ordered by guests the day before, and prepared by sous-chefs early in the morning) came with Wedgwood china and linen table cloths.

With such fine accommodation, wealthy sportsmen from across Eastern Canada and the United States began

Courtesy of Algonquin Park Museum

River ford; Hayes fishing party

to arrive in Algonquin park—and almost all wanted a fishing guide. Indeed, before 1930 a guide was considered essential if one wanted a successful fishing trip. The Hotel Algonquin and the Highland Inn built guide cabins. The Highland, because of its well-heeled clientele—some of whom thought nothing of tipping a

Courtesy of Algonquin Park Museum

Highland Inn in the 1920s

guide more than a day's wages—had some of the best woodsmen in the highlands virtually living there all summer.

Among those guides were men like Ralph and

Arthur Bice, brothers from the small village of Kearney, on the western edge of the park, who held the trapping rights for most of the township. There was John B. Whiteduck, from the Golden Lake Indian Reserve; Basil Sawyer from Whitney; and Jack Avery, whose family ran Opeongo Lodge for many decades. It was said of these men that they could catch fish in a bathtub.

The guides called their clients "Sports," a term of either affection or derision, the distinction depending on the personality of the individual Sport and the size of the tip. In the company of a good guide, the Sports had an opportunity to catch fish they could only dream about back home. In 1912, G. W. Collier of Bordenstown, New Jersey, won grand prize in a contest organized by *Field & Stream* magazine for a lake trout 30½ inches long, caught at Lake of Two Rivers. Two years later, park superintendent George Bartlett, in his annual report to the provincial government, stated: "Nearly all the prizes offered by sporting journals won this year were taken by fish from Algonquin Park."

Before long, Algonquin was where rich sportsmen from the northeastern seaboard came for their "Canadian vacation." Not until the 1930s did Canadian visitors begin to outnumber their American neighbours.

For the guides, the arrival of the Sports meant summer income. In the fall and winter they ran their traplines or worked in the lumber camps, but as soon as the ice went out in spring they returned with their canoes and

Hotel Algonquin in the 1920s

their tents to Algonquin park. Guiding never paid as well as trapping—one good fisher pelt might bring more at the fur auction in Toronto than an entire month of guiding. But the men were used to hard work, and to making money any way they could; so the arrival of the Sports was an unexpected, and welcome, source of extra income. The guides would fish in spring and summer, and when trout season closed they would return to their other jobs. Trapping, or bringing down pine, or doing survey work for the Department of Lands and Forests.

Just as Frank Kuiack had done.

While I was reading up on Algonquin park I was also making preparations for our fishing trip. Frank had waived his usual guiding fee—$150 a day—and I had agreed to cover all expenses: camping permits, food, gas

Woman with fishing gear, early 1900s

for the Dakota truck. Frank would supply the canoe and the fishing gear. All I had to bring were clothes, a sleeping bag and a tent.

Much of the planning had been done in an afternoon, sitting around Frank's kitchen table with a map of Algonquin park spread in front of us. We drank coffee, ate boiled-trout sandwiches and examined the map, the park a dark green, the canoe routes marked in pink, the lakes a robin's egg blue. The map was laminated, for people who spent a lot of time out on the water.

Like any good map, much of the history of the park was hinted at in the place names and symbols. There was the graveyard at Radiant Lake, the burial place of men who had died on log runs in the nineteenth century. Ralph Bice Lake was to the far western edge of the park. In the middle of the map was Opeongo Lake, so large it seemed to dominate the map. It was at Opeongo that Colonel John Dennison, one of the park's first settlers, was killed by a bear in 1881. You could still see the depot farm he cleared out of the wilderness, a slightly lighter shade of green just past the straits that led to the east arm of Opeongo. I looked at the map and wanted to go everywhere.

"What kind of fish will you be wantin' to catch?" asked Frank.

"Trout."

"We'll go after lake trout then. Try to catch a good one."

Courtesy of Algonquin Park Museum

Guide with packs, Hayes fishing party

I nodded and looked again at the map.

"We could go to Happy Isle," said Frank, pointing at a small lake on the map, just northwest of Opeongo Lake. "It might be busy, though. Lot of people take water taxis up Opeongo now. Real easy to get in to Happy Isle these days."

"Let's go someplace else, then."

"Do you want to break camp every day, or stay put and fish around?"

"I hadn't thought about that," I said. "Maybe it wouldn't be a bad idea to stay in one place. Fish around? You mean go to other lakes?"

"Right on. We camp on one lake, and go fish some others. Fish around."

"Let's do that."

"Maybe go to Ragged Lake then," said Frank, pointing to a lake south of Highway 60, on the west side of the park. "Good lake trout at Ragged, and there's lots of good lakes right around it. Bonnechere. Big Porcupine. Could fish a different lake every day."

I looked at the lake Frank was pointing at, a large lake with many bays, inlets and channels. Just the shape of it intrigued me.

"Let's go there," I said.

Whitney was teeming with tourists the morning I arrived. The heat was already oppressive, a surprisingly hot day after a wet, cold summer. When I pulled into

Frank's driveway I saw in the back of the Dakota a six-teen-foot fibreglass canoe, patched from bow to stern, including one long strip in the middle. Frank was sitting on the bottom rung of the fire escape, drinking coffee and waiting.

"Is this the canoe we're taking?" I asked.

"Right on."

I felt a heartbeat go missing.

"Frank, are you sure that canoe is going to work?"

"Been workin' fine for pret' near forty years. Do ya believe someone threw it out?"

I believed. The canoe, I would learn later, had once been owned by Camp Arowhon. When it showed up, split in two, at the dump at Lake of Two Rivers, someone phoned Frank—who practically has people on retainer at every municipal dump in the highlands—and he rescued the boat, brought it home and patched it up.

Frank has acquired dozens of canoes in this way: including nineteen that are cached on lakes throughout Algonquin park. The man hates to throw anything away.

The Eureka tent he brings on our trip was thrown away by campers at Pog Lake campground ("Nothin' wrong but a busted zipper"); his fishing poles were presented to him broken in pieces; his backpack is a Woods rucksack, bought thirty years ago. Hiking magazines may debate the benefits of an internal versus an external frame, but the Woods has neither. You throw it on your back, you start walking.

With Frank, there is never a conflict between form and function. There is only function. Who needs Mountain Equipment Co-op fashion when you can buy work clothes and a rain poncho at the Stedmans in Bancroft? Who needs dehydrated food when McCain's makes instant mashed potatoes? And who needs a two-thousand-dollar Kevlar canoe when someone threw away a perfectly good fibreglass one—only busted in two—forty years ago?

"It may not look like much," said Frank, "but it's a good canoe. When the wind comes up I'd rather have this canoe 'stead of those lightweight Kevlar ones with no keel. Those canoes will kill ya."

I decided not to mention the canoe again. Besides, it wasn't like I was going to back out. I was committed. If Frank had shown up with a rubber dinghy I would have gone on the trip in a rubber dinghy.

After coffee I threw my gear in the back of the Dakota and we headed off to the park. There seemed to be as many people arriving that day as leaving, even though a long weekend was coming to an end. At the Canoe Lake Access Store we had to stand in line to get our camping permit. In the store was a display of a "typical" Algonquin park campsite from "bygone days." The packsack in the display looked newer than Frank's. I pointed it out to him. "Good pack," he said.

After unloading the gear and parking the Dakota we made our way down Smoke Lake, a large, beautiful lake named because of the mist that rises from the water every morning—so much mist that it looks like smoke from a forest fire. Along the shore of the lake were many cottages, most of them quite old—the park hasn't given out a land lease in nearly fifty years. And you can't buy the land. The only new cottages had replaced existing cottages that had burned down or fallen apart. Given the grandeur of the new cottages, the fate of the former cabins seemed a great convenience.

Although there had been plenty of clues the fishing trip I was about to go on would be different from any other I had taken—the patched-up canoe, the Woods rucksacks, people's stares when we set off down Smoke, Frank dressed in his dark-green work clothes with a hand-rolled cigarette dangling from his mouth—it was only at the portage that I understood just how different.

When guiding fishing parties was a regular job for the men of the highlands, they did everything for the client—paddled the canoes, cooked the meals, cleaned the fish, everything. And so, at the portage, Frank insisted on carrying the canoe and most of the gear. I was allowed to carry only one pack (which was fortunate because my legs buckled when I tried to put it on).

When Frank had hoisted the canoe on his shoulders I asked how much it weighed—eighty-nine pounds it turned out, almost double the weight of a new fibreglass canoe. And all Frank said was, "Can't beat the price."

With that he began walking. Once I had my pack on I tried to catch up, but only caught glimpses of his back through the forest. He passed me on the trail when he was doubling back to get the rest of the gear.

At the end of the portage we rested not far from an old lumber dam. There had been a wooden chute the other side of the dam, where logs were sent down from Ragged to Smoke, and we walked down a short trail to find it. You had to look hard, as most of the wood had washed away and the remaining pieces were rotted and overgrown with moss and lichen. Except for the metal dam above us, and those few pieces of wood, you never would have known a log chute had once been there.

We paddled down Ragged Lake to our campsite in late afternoon, as the sun inched toward the treeline. The campsite was on a point that would give us unobstructed views of both sunrises and sunsets. After we unloaded the gear I wasn't allowed to do anything more than pitch my tent. Just as well. When I took the tent out of the bag I discovered one of the poles was broken. I decided to set it up anyway. It didn't look like it was going to rain that night, so a slightly sagging tent wouldn't be the end of the world.

Frank shook his head and walked off. Two minutes later he was back, carrying a small spruce bough. With his Buck knife he whittled both ends of the bough, then neatly inserted it into the assembled ridge pole, in place of the busted piece. I stood embarrassed and silent,

Photo by Julie Oliver

briefly wondering why people like me bothered with manufactured poles in the first place.

There was another problem when Frank discovered the firepit grill was missing. We scoured the campsite but couldn't find it. I knew we could build a wooden grill if needed, but Frank had other ideas. He paddled to a nearby island and returned, not ten minutes later, with a small, metal grill.

"How in the world did you get that?"

"Oh, I had it hidden over there," said Frank. "Found it once and thought I might need it one day."

I looked at the grill's circular shape, and knew that no barbecue had been manufactured like that for decades.

"How long has it been hidden for?"

"Oh, a few years."

After that Frank started supper. I sat on the granite outcrop, watching as he worked. I timed him: he squared and split a twenty-foot cedar log in five minutes twenty-eight seconds, then started a fire, got it raging, in forty-two seconds. When the coals were to his liking, Frank placed several ground meat patties in an aluminum frying pan, mixed mashed potatoes in a small pot, and before long called me for dinner.

"This is delicious," I said, as we ate by the fire, the plastic dinner plates balanced on our knees. "What kind of meat is it?"

"Moose."

"I've never had moose before. Where did you get it?"

"In the park."

"You can't hunt in the park."

"Didn't. They phoned me up. They always phone me up. I'm the only one that bothers to come out any more. Nobody wants to work. Good moose. Weighed 845 pounds dressed out."

"What do you mean they phoned you up?"

"Whenever a moose gets hit on the highway they phone me and I come take it away. Get a lot of moose that way."

I looked at my plate. My God, it was roadkill.

Frank
and Marie

Frank's education started at the age of ten. He went to the Airy Public School, even though the Kuiacks were staunch Catholics and there was a Catholic school in Whitney. The decision was a practical one: the public school was two miles closer than the Catholic school.

Frank would do his chores—water and milk the cows, feed the pigs—then walk the mile and a half to school. Along the way he was joined by the other children of Slab Town—his cousins, Lawrence and Raymond Kuiack; Charlie Levine; Elmer and Marlene Bolt; Shirley Close. The group would trudge down the railway line and cross the new highway to the one-room schoolhouse built on a small hill surrounded by hardwood trees.

The school was made of whitewashed, hewn lumber,

with a wood stove at the front of the room, six large slate boards on the front and left wall, and windows on the right-hand wall just too high to look out of when you were seated at your desk. Frank's first teacher was fired halfway through the school year after she was caught stealing pencils from the students. During recess the pencils would disappear and the teacher, accusing the children of being negligent, would insist they bring a penny from home before they would be given a new one.

Although many of the parents in Slab Town were indignant at the teacher's behaviour, Frank didn't have any strong feelings about it. He figured the teacher was just doing what everyone was doing around Whitney, trying to get by as best she could. Besides, why should folks be angrier at the teacher than any other poacher—his father had hidden any number of them in the family home when they would knock late at night saying the park rangers were right behind them.

He just didn't want to keep buying pencils.

The next teacher, Mrs. Hunter, was less entrepreneurial and paid special attention to Frank. In time he came to enjoy the writing and reading lessons. He knew he had to learn English, knew that it would take work and he didn't mind doing it. Still, he never cared for the one-room schoolhouse—the windows you couldn't see out of, the dusty smell of chalk and the giggling and whispering of his classmates. He looked forward to the days of deep winter, when it was too cold to walk to school: the trestle bridge over Long Lake becoming impassable, the wind at that height adding twenty negative degrees to the land temperature. When he awoke on a cold winter day he would check the water pail in the kitchen before doing his chores: if the water was frozen, he would be staying home.

On frozen-water-pail days he would hurry through his chores and sit next to the wood stove in the front room reading books Mrs. Hunter had lent him: *Huckleberry Finn, Tales of King Arthur,* novels by Louis L'Amour and Zane Grey, who was perhaps his favourite writer. Grey's tales of cowboys and Plains Indians were so vivid that he often dreamed about them, although he had trouble imagining the land they inhabited and tended to substitute blue, cold rivers for the sluggish, brown Mississippi; stands of hemlock and tamarack for the Great Plains; fishing guides for cowboys.

Frank thought of fishing guides the way other boys thought of cowboys or hockey players or knights errant. In his dreams he would take rich fishing parties into the interior of Algonquin park. They would fish from canoes, not rowboats, for trout, not bass. The men in the fishing party would seek his advice, treat him with respect, the way Sports treated Basil Sawyer and the Lavallys and the Luckasavitches.

Rich men would congratulate him on the fine fishing trip, stuff wadded bills into his pocket and invite him to their homes in the States after trout season. The women who had been kept comfortable at night in canvas tents, with cheesecloth spread across the flap to keep away mosquitoes, would also thank him for such a pleasant trip. Other guides would say it was a good idea to fish the shoal on the far bay of the lake, not all that good this time of year, but somehow Frank knew there would be fish.

For the most part, though, his dreams were of catching fish. The lake would always be flat calm, a hot summer day without wind. The shoreline would be differing shades of dark green, always spruce and pine, never hardwoods for some reason. The trout would break the surface of the lake, twisting and jerking on the line, water splaying off in intricate waterfall patterns. The fishing party would catch trout all day, pulling the fish from the water like silver coins plucked from a wishing well.

"I've never caught so many fish," a delighted American would say.

"Should have been here a week ago," Frank answered. "We were throwing back ten-pounders."

The man would stare at Frank in amazement, and disappear as another dream started. This time, Frank was fishing with a tall, thin man smoking a pipe. The man wore a black toque and a plaid shirt. They were friends, Frank and this man, and people stared at both of them with respect.

National Gallery of Canada, Ottawa

Tom Thomson fishing at Tea Lake dam, circa 1913–1914

"Do you want to try our special spot?" the man would say.

"Sure, Tom."

And they would paddle down the lake, to a place known only to them. In his sleep Frank would smile. He was dream-fishing with the most famous guide of them all.

Tom Thomson, the painter of such Canadian icons as *Northern River* and *Jack Pine*, first came to Algonquin park in the spring of 1912. The thirty-four-year-old native of Owen Sound was then working at Grip Limited, a commercial design firm in Toronto, which also employed five of the future members of the Group of Seven—J. E. H. MacDonald, Arthur Lismer, Franklin Carmichael, Frank Johnston and Fred Varley.

In their company Thomson, who had no formal training, became enamoured of the artist's life. At the urging of Varley, who had made a trek to the highlands the year before, Thomson came to the park on a sketching trip with his friend Ben Jackson. He stayed for several weeks at Tea Lake. (A sketch done at the time by Jackson, called *Rainy Day at Camp* and now in the National Gallery, shows Thomson fishing by the shore of Tea Lake, a rod in his hand, his ever-present pipe in his mouth. Virtually every sketch or photo taken of Thomson in Algonquin park shows him either fishing or posed in front of the day's catch. Painting he did in solitude.)

Those weeks on Tea Lake in 1912 changed not only Thomson's life, but the course of Canadian art. The following spring Thomson sold a painting called *A Northern Lake*, made from a sketch he had done that same summer just north of Algonquin, at a showing of the Ontario Society of Artists. The Ontario government purchased the painting, for the then princely sum of $250. Suddenly, Thomson was a real painter.

(A popular story about Thomson says that upon receiving his cheque he cashed it at a bank, insisting upon being paid in one-dollar bills. He then spent a rowdy, drunken night with friends, tossing the bills in the air and letting them rain down on his head.)

The following spring Thomson returned to Algonquin park, staying at Mowat Lodge—on Canoe Lake—run by Shannon Fraser and his wife, Annie. The Mowat was primarily a fishing lodge, and Fraser always had trouble keeping good guides because of competition from "hoity-toity" lodges like the Highland Inn. When he discovered his guest from Toronto was a skilled trout fisherman, he asked Thomson if he wanted to guide. Thomson, who never had much money, accepted gladly.

And so Tom Thomson became a fishing guide much in demand by guests at the Mowat Lodge. Although a guide from Toronto would normally be the butt of laughter and scorn among local guides, Thomson wasn't. His unassuming manner—unlike most city folks—was something the guides could respect and identify with. He was also, no way you could deny it, a damn good fisherman.

In his diaries, Chief Ranger Mark Robinson, who became a friend, wrote how Thomson "would catch trout where other guides said it was impossible." Part of his success was due to the flies and lures he made. It was not uncommon for Thomson to spend an entire day on Canoe Lake, watching to see what insects and water nymphs the trout were feeding on. Then he would go back to the lodge, mix up some paint, and replicate the insects to perfection.

It was Thomson's unerring, and brazen, use of colour that made him a great artist. He had little interest in the lush, uniformly green forests of the Algonquin countryside in summer, or its wide, unmarked expanses of winter snow (which most inspired his close friend, and Group of Seven member, A. Y. Jackson). Thomson preferred working in the seasons of colour—spring and fall.

Tale after tale has been told of Thomson's obsession with getting the colour just right. Once, a guest at Mowat Lodge watched as Thomson painted the same yellow birch, morning after morning, for several weeks. Finally the guest asked Thomson if she could see the painting. Thomson replied there was no painting. He was merely mixing paint in an effort to match the birch bark as it changed colour during the spring.

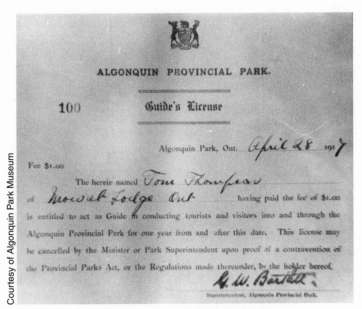

Tom Thomson's guide licence.
His name was misspelt by Chief Ranger Mark Robinson.

Another story is told of Thomson's canoe, which he purchased in Huntsville. For reasons he never explained, Thomson was determined to paint the canoe a particular dove grey, which he set about mixing. For weeks, guests at Mowat Lodge watched as Thomson spent every evening mixing and remixing paint in an effort to get the colour right. Finally, he announced to the bemused guests that he had done it—he had his dove-grey canoe. He had also spent all his money on paint.

His obsession with colour turned out to be that of a genius. In his short career Thomson transformed Canadian landscape painting with a distinctive impressionistic style that one critic at the time dismissed as "moods smudged into panels." It didn't matter. It worked. *Jack Pine*, showing a gnarled tree leaning over an Algonquin lake, weather-beaten, yet somehow majestic—an effect aided by Thomson's brazen use of purple and orange—may be the most famous painting ever done by a Canadian.

His use of colour was so inventive that many of his artist friends in Toronto were convinced Thomson had "made it up." Only when they visited Algonquin park themselves could they appreciate the truthfulness of his work. And with that discovery, all the rules changed. Thomson masterpieces such as *The West Wind* and *Northern River* not only cemented his reputation as a visionary artist but left their mark on generations to follow.

Such fame and influence, however, would come after his death. Thomson drowned while fishing on Canoe Lake on July 8, 1917, long before his reputation had been established.

On that day guests at Mowat Lodge watched Thomson load his dove-grey canoe with fishing gear, a pack and some food, and head out on the lake. Although Thomson told no one where he was headed, Robinson long suspected he was going to Gill Lake, a small, nearly inaccessible lake southwest of Canoe Lake that was known for its large trout. Thomson and Robinson had a friendly wager going at the time, on a large Canoe Lake trout that both men had hooked and lost. Thomson had told Annie Fraser that morning that he was going to catch a huge lake trout and leave it at Robinson's front door, to imply he had just won the bet.

When he did not return that night, no one at the lodge, or around Canoe Lake, was overly concerned. Thomson could disappear for days at a time, bringing with him no more gear than what he had loaded into his canoe that afternoon. Not even the sighting of a swamped canoe drifting by Wapomeo Island that after-noon was cause for concern. A canoe had drifted from the Mowat Lodge dock the night before, and it was assumed to be the same one.

Two days later the canoe was again spotted drifting by Wapomeo Island; this time its distinctive dove-grey colouring was noticed by a cottager who knew Thomson. A search began that day, led by Robinson. Apparently believing his friend was too good a canoeist to have drowned, Robinson concentrated his search on land, checking out the portage to Gill Lake, the shore-line of Canoe Lake and various other portages in the area. Perhaps Thomson was injured and waiting for help to arrive.

On Monday, July 16, two guides from Mowat Lodge were paddling by Wapomeo Island when they saw an object come to the surface. It was Thomson's body. One guide stayed with the body while the other went to park headquarters to notify the authorities. Superintendent George Bartlett dispatched Robinson to stay with the body until the coroner could arrive from North Bay. Robinson took provisions for a night's stay and made his way to the island.

With Thomson's body laid out on a granite outcrop, Robinson and the guides spent the night huddled before a small fire. It was a clear night, with a strong wind licking through the birch and the poplar, the only sounds— for who would speak at such a time?—being the waves lapping on the shore. Thomson's body was covered with a blanket and tied to a tree.

When the coroner did not arrive the next morning, the body was taken to the nearby cottage of Dr. G. W. Howland, who carried out an examination. There was a four-inch-long bruise on Thomson's left temple. In his diary, Robinson wrote that the bruise was likely caused by falling on a rock. By this time two undertakers from Huntsville had arrived. Dr. Howland advised burying the body as soon as possible.

Thomson was laid to rest in a small cemetery on Canoe Lake that afternoon. Later in the day the coroner finally arrived and held an inquest without ever seeing the body. He ruled it an accidental death by drowning. The following day the Thomson family sent a telegram, requesting that the body be returned to them in Owen

National Gallery of Canada, Ottawa

Tom Thomson with the day's catch,
Canoe Lake, circa 1915

Sound. That night another undertaker arrived from Huntsville and exhumed Thomson's body, placed it in a new casket and shipped it out on the morning train.

The coroner never hazarded a guess on how, or why, Thomson had drowned. It was assumed he had either had a heart attack, or had stumbled, fatally, at the beginning of the portage to Gill Lake. Some locals, however, speculated right from the start that he had been murdered, perhaps by cottager Martin Blecher, a rival of Thomson's for the affections of a young woman living on Canoe Lake.

Nearly forty years later, a body was found in Thomson's first grave on Canoe Lake. By then, Thomson's fame was such that the discovery became front-page news across the country. The body was exhumed and shipped to Toronto for forensic examination where it was determined to be a young Aboriginal male, and not Thomson. The fact that the body had a small hole in the left temple, and that the casket exactly matched the description of the one in which Thomson was initially buried, ensured the forensic findings were hotly debated, and continue to be so.

Shortly after his death, a cairn was constructed on Wapomeo Island in Thomson's honour by his Toronto friends, J. W. Beatty and J. E. H. MacDonald. The inscription reads:

To the memory of Tom Thomson: Artist; woodsman; guide; who was drowned in Canoe Lake, July 8th, 1917. He lived humbly but passionately with the wild—it made him brother to all untamed things of nature. It drew him apart and revealed itself wonderfully to him. It sent him out

*from the woods only to show these revelations
through his art—and it took him to itself at last.*

Frank Kuiack had visited the cairn and thought it the
most wonderful thing he had ever seen. A monument to
a fishing guide. Something holy.

Frank awoke in his bunk, blinking his eyes and slowly
realizing he was no longer the head guide on a
Highland Inn fishing trip in Algonquin park, nor the
friend of Tom Thomson. He was a bull cook at the
McRae Lumber camp on Perieau Lake, and it was the
winter of 1950.

He pulled on his boots, then a wool sweater, a heavy
flannel jacket, and went outside. The sun had yet to
break the treeline and the sky was filled with stars. He
gathered the pails by the stairs of the bunkhouse and
started to walk to the lake. The cooks would be up in
half an hour and he had to have the water ready, the
fire going.

Frank had attended the Airy Public School until the
previous spring, when he had completed Grade 8 and
there was no sense going any further because it would
have meant travelling to the village of Madawaska, and
it was mostly girls that went to the school in
Madawaska, certainly none of the Kuiack boys. Besides,
he could read and write, understood enough math to get
by, and the purpose of school had been realized.

McRae lumber camp on Lake of Two Rivers, 1942

He had gone into the lumber camp with his father and Edmund that autumn, shortly after his fourteenth birthday. If not for his father, who had worked for McRae for years, he never would have got the job. He was small even for his age, and as it was he couldn't work with the men, felling trees and hauling them out of the bush. He was the bull cook, his job to haul water and wood for the cooks; clean out the stables and the pig barns; anything else the real cooks and shantymen didn't want to do. He was paid $3.20 a day.

74

It was at Perieau Lake that Frank saw his first chain-saw, a deadly, four-foot-long implement that required two men to operate, one in the back and the one who lost the coin toss in front, guiding the teeth with a small metal handhold. There was no carburetor and the saw was as loud as a passing train.

Frank's father took one look at the saw and spat on the ground in contempt.

"Who would invent such a thing?" he asked his youngest son. "We should throw it in the lake."

When the chainsaw disappeared two days later, Frank just smiled and went about his work. He thought his father was right: "Who would invent such a thing?" There was enough noise in the camp as there was—between the shouts and curses of the loggers, trees crashing to the ground, mules braying, pigs squealing—the last thing needed was more noise.

In the spring he went back to guiding fishermen from the States around Long Lake. No longer a boy, he was by now accepting the silver flasks of brandy and whisky when they were offered him. (His father owned a still and had supplied the McRae bush camps for years. He kept it hidden under the manure pile in the pig barn, the one place the Royal Canadian Mounted Police never looked when they knocked on the door late at night.)

Frank enjoyed the guiding trips on Long Lake as much as when he was a boy. Although he was only six-teen, he was already beginning to wonder why the events of a man's life kept getting in the way of what he wanted. School. The bush camp. He had asked for none of it, and yet there it was: his life. The life led and the life wanted, the distance between those two worlds, caused a surfacing of emotions in Frank he had never known before, the most pronounced and troublesome among them being regret. As a boy it had never existed. Then it was there, and it had never really disappeared since. He wondered if it was the same for everyone.

The next autumn he returned to the bush camp on Perieau Lake, this time with his best friend, Mervin Lagenskie, who because of his larger size was allowed to go into the woods, while Frank continued as bull cook. It was better now that Mervin was there; at least there was a friend to talk to in the evenings, and Mervin even helped, although he certainly didn't have to, with cleaning out the stables and barns at the end of the day.

Winter came late one night that year. The camp awoke on a mid-November morning to find six inches of freshly fallen snow, and it seemed for five months after that Frank barely slept. The timber limit McRae was working around Perieau Lake was nearly exhausted of pine and the company wanted it cleared that season, so there would be no wastage. The camp would be moved to another limit, in Algonquin park, the following year. In February the men even worked by the light of kerosene lamps, while Frank kept the cook fires burning.

That April, near the end of the season, Frank and Mervin were in the pig stables, shovelling manure, when Mervin said:

"Frankie, why are we working at this bush camp for peanuts? I bet McRae doesn't even know our names."

"Of course he doesn't know our names," laughed Frank. "That pig over there, the one he paid money for and that will feed his men, if that pig had a name he'd know it. Why would he know ours? We're just the bushmen."

"Actually, I'm a bushman," said Mervin. "You're just the bull cook."

Frank flung a shovel of shit at Mervin's head but his friend ducked and the shit landed harmlessly on the walls of the stable. It slid down the rough-hewn pine boards and landed on the snow.

"Listen, Frank," said Mervin, after he had stopped laughing, "I know your father owes McRae something. He's worked for him his whole life and everybody loves your dad. McRae will always take care of him. But why are we here? This has been a bitch of a winter and the money we're going to make from it is no better than that shit you just threw at me."

"What else can we do?" asked Frank.

"I know where we can make some real money."

"Where?"

Mervin looked at him and kicked away a pig that had begun sniffing at his ankles.

"Timmins. I hear you can make a fortune there in the gold mines."

Frank looked around the pig barn and said:

"All right. Let's go."

They caught the Ontario Northlands bus out of Barry's Bay, but on the way to Timmins were told that work could be had on a highway being built to Elliot Lake. So they got off the bus at Sudbury and walked to a Department of Highways office to sign up. For six months Frank and Mervin spread gravel behind a convoy of dumpsters making their way slowly toward Elliot Lake and the mines that were about to open.

The land was as rugged as back home, Frank decided, had the same hills and pines and fast-moving rivers, but there were no hardwood trees and none of the colour and variety of the Algonquin Highlands. It was a lush, uniformly green land, although once, when they had stopped for lunch and a bull moose had wandered out of the forest, he felt right at home, wishing for a moment he had his 300 Savage.

When the road was completed they collected their last pay and continued on to Timmins, where they got jobs at Dome Mines. The foreman at the company trailer asked their ages and they both lied:

"Eighteen," Mervin said.

"And you?"

"I'm eighteen too."

"You're a bit small for eighteen."

"I'm bigger than my dad, and he's a lot older than eighteen."

The foreman sniffed and looked down at Frank.

"Your dad a good worker?"

"He's a foreman himself. At McRae's Lumber in Whitney, Ontario. He'd outwork you, I bet."

The foreman gave them both a time card. Their shift started at six in the morning the next day, when the miners would line up before the metal elevator cages, punch a clock, and then travel down to where they would work for the day, sometimes as far as 2,800 feet below the surface. They would use air drills and shovels to dig out the rock, then load the stone into mucking machines which would take the cargo to the mine's main station. There it would be loaded into boxcars and conveyor belts and taken to the surface. Up top, the rock would be sent though a crusher and then sifted for gold.

It would have been difficult to imagine a place more different from the hills and lakes of the Algonquin Highlands. In the mine shaft Frank found it hard to breathe, hard to think with the constant shouts of the miners and the metal-on-rock cacophony of the work. Once, while working by himself on a vein deep in the shaft, his light failed and he sat calling for help in the tunnel. Most people think they know darkness—turn off your bedroom light, walk a country lane late at night, you think you know dark—but true dark is not visual. True dark smothers you with its touch; it has a smell you can't forget, a fear that lingers for years.

Frank began drinking heavily in Timmins. There was moonshine for sale in the Dome Mines bunk-houses, and every second Friday the men would crowd into the bars and taverns of Timmins, to drink their wages until they passed out or were escorted back to the bunkhouses by the Ontario Provincial Police. It was on just such a drinking spree that he met his wife, Barbara. They spent a heavy night drinking at the Maple Leaf Tavern, making drunken promises of love, devotion and marriage, both of them surprised when they ended up at the offices of the Justice of the Peace the next day and delivered on one of the promises. They were both six-teen. They moved into a rented home on the outskirts of Timmins. Later that year a son was born; the next year, another son.

There were soon problems, drunken fights over money and children, and Frank started working extra shifts at the mine to avoid going home. Three years after they were married Frank returned from work and found the house empty, except for a sheetless double bed and some of his mining clothes. He thought briefly of trying to track Barbara down, but then started drinking instead. The boys would be better off, he reasoned. He was still a teenager.

Mervin returned to Whitney shortly afterwards, his enthusiasm for the money to be made in Timmins thoroughly exhausted by the reality of the work. Frank thought of joining him, but steady drinking had made him indecisive. Every once in a while, when he wasn't drinking—in the mine shaft early in the morning, or in his unfurnished house late at night—he would think about his days as a fishing guide in Whitney. It had been eleven years now since the men from Ohio had first asked him to row around Long Lake and show them the good spots. He would have liked that as a life, even though it wasn't the way it once was.

The Highland Inn hired few fishing guides any more, and who would have thought that day would come? The Highland even looked worn out these days. A lot of people coming to the park stayed in the new autocamps, leaving the inn sitting there half-empty some nights, even in August. It was the same way at the Hotel Algonquin.

They paved the highway through the park too. Now people could drive right in to Lake of Two Rivers, throw a boat in the water and fish, just as easy as you please. There were enough fish in the lakes along the new paved highway that even a poor fisherman could catch his limit. There just wasn't the demand for guides any more. Unless you were serious about fishing, unless you knew it would go better with a guide—but how many people were serious any more?

It would have been enough to return to Whitney as often as he could for extended fishing trips, bringing nothing but a canoe, an axe, a canvas tarp, a Zippo lighter and his fishing rod. Camped beneath a white pine, in front of a fire, it seemed for a while that the drunken fights with Barbara had happened to another man, and the mine shaft was something he had only dreamed.

After one of his fishing trips, heading back to the mines, his bus stopped at North Bay. He got out to stretch his legs. It was a beautiful night. No wind. The stars spread across the sky like falling snow. When they called the passengers back onto the bus a woman lined up behind him. She was astonishingly short and he remembered wondering: four foot ten? Four foot nine?

They ended up sitting next to each other. He asked her name. She answered, "Marie."

Her full name was Marie Wabi—half French Canadian, half Ojibwa. Frank followed her off the bus in Cobalt and asked if he could take her out for dinner. When they were seated at a booth in the diner, Frank asked and she gave him an honest answer: four foot ten.

She had short, black, curly hair and blue eyes that stared straight into his when he talked, not hesitant or uncertain. She had been married twice. Her first husband was a fishing guide who died when a float plane crashed in the Ottawa River. The second was a truck driver who had gone on a long-distance haul the year before last and hadn't been back. She had eleven children.

"Order anything you want," Frank said, trying to show off. "I have money."

She ordered steak.

"How would you like it cooked?"

Well done.

Frank motioned for the waitress, ordered two steaks, one well done, the other medium rare, and two beers. When the beer came he sent the waitress back for a glass, and then poured one beer into it. He gave it too much head and blushed, waiting for the beer to settle before handing it to Marie.

"You must be on your way to the mines," she said.

"That's right," he answered. "How did you know?"

"A lot of the miners take the bus. And you look like one."

"I'm not a miner. I hate it."

"Not many like it. But they're miners just the same."

"I'm doing it for the money. And then I'm moving on."

She sipped her beer and looked at him.

"Where will you go?"

"I haven't decided yet. Maybe out west."

Frank flipped through the metal song cards in the jukebox on their table, avoiding her eyes. He pulled a dime from his pocket, slid it in the slot, and punched an Earl Scruggs song.

"Where are you from, then?" she asked, her fingers tapping the rhythm of the song on the Formica tabletop.

"Whitney, just outside Algonquin park. Have you ever been there?"

She shook her head. "What's it like?"

"Well, it's beautiful. There are lakes everywhere—I was raised on a lake—and forests you can get lost in for months. I know the bush around there 'bout as good as any man, I figure. That's where I'm coming back from now."

"You go home often?"

"Often as I can."

Their steak arrived and Frank ordered two more beers. When Marie cut into her steak, the meat was a light, mauve colour. Frank put down his fork.

"You wanted it well done, right?"

She nodded her head.

"Well, that's not well done. Not by a long shot."

"It's all right."

"No, it's not."

The beer arrived and Frank sent the steak back to the kitchen. Marie blushed and said thank you.

"You didn't have to do that, Frank. It's nice of you to take me out to supper, but the steak was fine."

"It weren't the way you wanted it. I'm a cook myself, or used to be, at a lumber camp," and he lied some more, the bull cook suddenly becoming the camp cook, Frank an expert on cooking steak, explaining how to do it right. She knew he was boasting, but let him go ahead. There was no harm in it. And he was nervous. She knew that as well. She was ten years older than Frank and understood things he had yet to think about.

When he had asked if he could take her out to dinner she was going to say no, because of his age, but the expression on his face had been so earnest she found herself saying yes. One dinner. What was the harm? Besides, she was hungry.

"You should start eating your steak," she said. "No sense it getting cold."

"I'll wait for you, don't be silly."

She smiled and looked down at her hands resting on the Formica. Silly. As if, the youngest child in a family of fourteen, the mother of eleven, she had ever had the time to be silly. She took no offence, though, understood the gesture for what it was.

The steak was brought back to the table and Marie thanked the waitress, who didn't answer. This time the meat was a dark, purple colour, almost black, the colour of blood that had hardened and congealed outside. A well-done steak.

Frank snorted contemptuously.

"Gawd, it's still purple."

"Frank, it's fine."

"No, it ain't."

He picked up her plate and walked toward the swinging doors of the kitchen. The waitress came from behind the counter and said, "Is there something I can help you with?"

"Apparently not," said Frank and kept on walking. The cook, a big, burly man with a snot- and blood-encrusted apron, looked up from the grill and asked Frank what he was doing.

"I'm going to cook my girl a steak."

He said it loud enough for Marie to hear and she blushed again, although she thought "my girl" was rather funny. He was like a boastful boy. The cook looked at Frank, thought about it for a second, and said, "Suit yourself, Bud."

Frank slapped the steak on the grill, picked up a spatula and pressed down hard, scouring the underside as flames licked up around his hands. He looked out the pickup window of the kitchen, waved at Marie, and then felt a sudden rush of heat. He pulled his hand back quickly, then looked up to see if Marie had noticed.

He switched the spatula to his left hand, and pressed his singed right hand against his leg, praying for the pain to go away.

Out in the diner, Marie noticed people had gone back to talking or reading the newspaper, no longer interested in Frank. She slowly raised her hand in front of her chest and waved back. She hoped his hand was not badly burned.

Most of Marie's children had already left home, but five boys still lived with her in Cobalt. That first night Frank slept on Marie's couch, sharing it with Michael, the youngest boy. Marie gave Frank a large Hudson's Bay blanket from her bed and said he could use that. It would be cold that night. He said the cold didn't bother him, and he wasn't going to take her blanket; but she insisted, convincing him by saying the blanket would be a treat for Michael, who usually slept under bedsheets and sweaters.

Marie thanked him again for supper.

"It weren't nothing," said Frank. "I'm just sorry you had to wait so long for your steak to be cooked right."

"It was fine in the end. Just perfect."

"Darn right it was. Hell, I should go to that diner tomorrow and take that cook's job away. Show 'em how to cook food in this town."

"It wouldn't surprise me if you did that."

She smiled at how easy it was to make Frank blush. Then she went to her bedroom, kissing him on the cheek and reminding him that the bus to Timmins left Cobalt at 8 A.M.

The next morning Frank feigned sleep, even after Michael pulled the blanket off the couch. Even after Marie had made a breakfast of porridge and toast for the children. Even after the front door had been opened and banged shut several times with children departing for school. When his watch showed 8:15, Frank stretched, yawned, rubbed his eyes, looked again at his watch, and shouted, "My Gawd, look at the time!"

Marie made him breakfast. She fried strips of salted

pork and her last two eggs, and made a pot of strong coffee. Frank said he would try to catch a ride out of Cobalt that afternoon, but first he was going to buy groceries.

"I'm not going to eat and run, leaving you with no food in the house," he said. She didn't argue for long. She already knew it was pointless. Besides she had a healthy respect for food and wasn't going to say she didn't need any when she did. Now, *that* would have been silly.

Frank spent more than fifty dollars that afternoon. At the butcher's he bought a full ham, ten pounds of bacon, some pork chops, a pot roast that would feed a woman and five boys, and there'd be leftovers. At the market he bought twenty pounds of potatoes, beets, carrots and onions; at the grocery, milk, eggs, cheese; at the bakery, pies and bread. They drove around Cobalt in a taxi. By mid-afternoon it didn't seem right, Frank buying so many groceries and then leaving town, so Marie invited him for supper. He could catch the bus the following morning. Frank said all right, but only if he cooked.

He stayed for ten days, acting surprised every morning when he got off the couch and looked at his watch, Marie always saying she didn't have the heart to wake him, and my Lord she never met a sounder sleeper. He took Michael fishing and he caught a ten-pound pike. Marie cooked it up and Frank had to admit it was pretty good. As a rule, he hated pike. But Marie was from up north, and knew how to cook it. Frank was impressed.

On the day he finally left Cobalt, Frank bought a ticket at the bus station and then sat outside on his duffel bag, waiting for the bus. More than forty years later, when he was done with raising children, when he had lived a full life, good years and bad, the no-longer-young man who had sat on that duffel bag outside the Cobalt bus station on the morning of May 13, 1954, will conclude there are few moments of true clarity in life.

But that was one of them. He still remembers the clarity he had that morning, as though the bus station were bathed in a harsh, white light that didn't allow for shadows and any decision you made was going to be the right one. The decision he made that morning was one of the easiest he ever made.

He finished his coffee, walked to the ticket window and told the Greyhound agent he wanted his ticket to Timmins exchanged for one to Barry's Bay. He pocketed the $2.35 difference in fare and went back to sitting on the duffel bag, waiting for the next bus south.

Fishing
PART II

The first morning on Ragged Lake I wasted little time in getting out of my tent. I had purchased it nearly twenty years ago, a gull-winged backpacking tent, at an outfitter's shop in Jasper, Alberta. It had not been set up in more than a decade, and there was a pungent smell to it. If the day looked good, with no threat of rain, I was going to take off the fly and air it out. The sleeping bag was going to be hung as well.

I put on my boots and joined Frank by the campfire, wondering what surprises might be in store for breakfast.

"Sleep well?" he asked.

"Slept wonderfully," I answered. "I think I was asleep the moment I got into my sleeping bag. Never woke up once."

Photo by Julie Oliver

Ragged Lake

That was rare, not getting up in the middle of the night. Back in Ottawa I would awake two or three times a night. Some nights when I couldn't get back to sleep I would watch infomercials until the sun came up, the newspapers were delivered and another day began. I had an appetite this morning, too, and that was equally strange.

There was a thick mist on the lake that morning, as if a large cumulus cloud had sat on the earth. We watched the mist slowly roll down the granite point, burning off the land first, until only the lake was shrouded. You could not see the shoreline across the strait, or the sun, or the loons calling from somewhere out on the water.

Frank was unloading pancake mix, bacon and eggs, getting ready to cook breakfast. Unless pigs got hit on the highway in Algonquin park, there would be no road-kill this morning. He put more maple logs on the fire, which would generate heat but not a large flame, perfect for cooking pancakes. He went into the woods behind the tents to gather more wood, and returned with an armload of maple and what looked to be a pine branch in the pocket of his jacket. He dropped the wood and took the pine from his pocket, which I now saw was a miniature tree.

"What's that?" I asked.

"Princess pine," said Frank. "I used to make money from these."

He put the tree on the ground and I looked at it. It was a perfect little pine tree, except for a large dry bud on top.

"You made money from that?"

"Oh, a lot of people made money from princess pine, not just me. There was a time when just about everyone in Whitney was picking it. After the war, we stripped the hills clean of the stuff."

"For what?"

"Sold 'em to Basil Sawyer."

"He was a guide, right?"

"Might have been one of the best guides ever," said

Frank. "His sons, Walter and Neil, still live in Whitney. I used to guide with Walter. He was the head guide at Hay Lake."

"So what did Basil Sawyer do with princess pine?"

"That's an interesting story."

And as Frank cooked breakfast that morning he told me the story of Basil Sawyer and princess pine, which is still told around Whitney, a good story, even fifty years later.

Basil Sawyer's grandfather, James Sawyer, came to Canada from Ireland in the mid-nineteenth century, first to Peterborough, Ontario, where he homesteaded, and then in 1870 to Hollow Lake, near Dorset, where the government was giving away larger tracts of land. He was one of the first settlers in the area. The other families left after a few years, realizing the land here would never support a farm, but Sawyer stayed and became a trapper. He had two sons, Benjamin and Hank, who built homes on Hollow Lake close to their father. Hank Sawyer had twelve children; the youngest, born in 1900, was Basil.

All of the Sawyer men were renowned bushmen, but it was acknowledged around Hollow Lake that there was something special about Basil. It wasn't just his size—in his early teens he was already six foot two and weighed more than two hundred pounds—there was also a certain felicity to him, an ability to outperform his peers with neither obvious effort nor boastfulness, that gave him a grace and popularity that should have been the envy of many, but wasn't.

When he was eighteen he started guiding, first around Hollow Lake, for the men who would arrive on the Grand Trunk Railway train from Buffalo, and then for the Highland Inn. When he was twenty-six he met Anona Mae McNeil, the newly arrived eighteen-year-old schoolteacher in Dorset. Although McNeil, from Leeds County in eastern Ontario, had once thought of marrying above her station—she had the schooling and physical good looks for such an ambition—she found herself falling in love with the handsome fishing guide from the Highland Inn. They were married at the United Church in Dorset the year they met.

Two years later, complaining it was getting "too crowded" on Hollow Lake, Basil and Anona moved to the other side of the park, to Jerusalem. They stayed only a year before deciding Jerusalem was also too crowded, and then they relocated, for good, to Paradise, along the shores of Hay Creek. They had five children—Walter, Durland, Neil, Arthur and Joy—and built a home from spruce logs McRae had left behind after closing a nearby sawmill.

Basil was given trapping rights for most of Clyde Township. He built a hunting cabin on McKenzie Lake that was almost as large as his home, and settled down. Life might have stayed as simple as that. And then he discovered princess pine.

It grows, almost like a weed, throughout Algonquin park, the surrounding highlands and much of northern Ontario. It never grows more than a foot tall, and is basically a miniature pine tree, a "scrub pine," as some call it. No one—not his sons, neighbours, nor the men around Whitney and Dorset who worked for him fifty years ago—can say for sure how Basil Sawyer found out about the man in Maynooth who was willing to pay for the miniature tree. One day he was ignorant; the next, Basil knew you could make money from princess pine. And to the man in front of the curve go the spoils.

So Basil, on those days when he was neither guiding nor hunting, began picking princess pine around Hay Creek, in the burns and hemlock stands where it grew best, then driving the bags of trees to Maynooth, where the man would purchase them for three cents a pound. Although secretive about the purpose, the man did own that he was selling the trees to an unnamed company in southern Ontario. One day, after Basil had been kept waiting at their agreed meeting place for four hours, he stormed into the CNR shipping office in Maynooth and demanded to know where the man was shipping his trees.

And thus Basil discovered the trees were being purchased by a company in Toronto, that was using them to make Christmas wreaths.

After that, the man from Maynooth was no longer needed. Basil began shipping the trees directly to

*Basil Sawyer, with lake trout caught
on Opeongo Lake*

Toronto. The company said this was fine with them, the man from Maynooth was a drunkard anyway. That first year Basil and his sons picked and shipped two tonnes of princess pine to Toronto. The next year Basil hired some neighbours on Hay Creek and shipped ten tonnes. Before long, any man in Whitney looking for extra money was picking princess pine and selling it to Basil, who now travelled around town in a stack-rail truck with a butcher's scale in the back, collecting burlap potato sacks stuffed with pine and handing out IOUs for money to be paid when the company in Toronto sent out the cheque. By 1949 he was shipping one hundred tonnes of princess pine a year to Toronto.

His wife, Anona, looked after the books for the Princess Pine Company of Whitney, Ontario, until the profits reached such a level that Basil thought it best he oversee the finances. Having no great skill at it, he had to work long hours on the books, poring through shipping invoices and freight bills and accounting ledgers wadded up with IOUs.

When the men around Whitney could not satisfy the demand for princess pine ("How many Christmas wreaths can they need?" Basil asked Walter one day), Basil started going farther afield, to Bancroft, Dorset and Huntsville, making weekly trips to buy scrub pine from out-of-work men and arranging for its shipment to Toronto. In time, he came up with the idea of buying most of his pine around North Bay, where there were plenty of burns, as well as a major railway terminus that could ship the trees directly to Toronto, thus cutting down on his freight and distribution costs. It was a smart business decision and Basil was pleased.

He kept guiding because the company in Toronto refused to buy trees in July and August, when the princess pine grew a large, wet bud that artificially inflated the weight. In September, when the bud had dried, he could start shipping again.

Before long he was thinking that the price paid for the pine by the company in Toronto—it had risen to twelve cents a pound—was not enough considering the obvious need for Christmas wreaths, and maybe there was a way to renegotiate the price. He also thought he needed more men in North Bay. He had yet to pick more pine than the company wanted, and maybe it was foolish not to test the market.

And so it was that Basil Sawyer drove to North Bay in the early summer of 1950 to arrange for the purchase and shipment of another load of princess pine. Although it was a sweltering day, he wore a recently purchased dark brown suit. By mid-morning the suit had dark stains under the arms and his white shirt was unfastened to the third button. Anona travelled beside him.

In North Bay he met the Hyland brothers, three Whitney men who had been picking princess pine in the burns of North Bay for two weeks, using kerosene lamps suspended on maple staffs so they could work at night and make as much money as possible before Basil showed up to arrange the last shipment of the season. They met at a tavern near the rail yards, where the Hylands had already stacked the burlap bags filled with pine. Basil had a beer and then went to inspect his trees—the bud had not sprouted yet; the bags were stuffed tight, no wastage—and he saw, by counting the pallets of pine stacked behind the station, that he would need an entire rail car for the shipment. He thought briefly of J. R. Booth, and how the old lumber baron used to travel in his own rail car up and down the upper Ottawa Valley and the Algonquin Highlands. Booth became one of the richest men in Canada at one time— and all from trees.

Basil went back to the tavern with the Hyland brothers while his wife went to a hotel. The men drank cold beer, laughed and told stories. They had made money together. Next year they would pick more princess pine, make more money. They talked of what they would purchase. Hunting cabins. New automobiles. Anona was going to be surprised with a Belanger cook stove that summer. They drank and laughed and enjoyed one another's company, these men who had made money together.

That night Basil ate a fine steak and slept soundly, although the next day, at the shipping office, he argued over a twenty-dollar discrepancy in the waybill, then fussed over the trees as they were loaded into the rail car.

It was another hot day. He said goodbye to the Hylands, assuring them they would be paid back in Whitney, when the cheque from Toronto arrived. He got into his stack-rail truck with the butcher's scale in the back and drove away from the North Bay railway station. The date was June 1, 1950.

There are some who say you should make nothing of what happened next. Basil's son, Durland, had the same thing happen to him, coming out of a portage on Shirley Lake, and Joy, didn't it happen to his daughter as well, when she was lined up at a movie theatre in Oshawa? People don't talk about them to this day. Why talk about Basil?

But then there are the others who say that is exactly why people still talk about it, because Basil Sawyer wasn't felled coming out of a portage on Shirley Lake; if he had, there might have been some revealing, or unfolding, of things that was logical. He had spent his life in the bush. If the best fishing guide to ever work in Algonquin park died on a portage, that would have made sense.

As it was, there was something out of place about it all, not like an explosion on a quiet day, something just slightly out of place: like waking up in a strange room; or seeing a child in a hospital bed.

It was a good thing Anona was there when Basil had his heart attack. Although she hadn't learned to drive she

Photo courtesy of Walter Sawyer

Wedding photo of Basil Sawyer and Anona McNeil

helped steer the truck off the highway and into the parking lot at the Burk's Falls hospital, Basil clutching his
chest and muttering "son of a bitch." If it weren't for

Anona, Basil likely would have driven off the highway and been killed instantly, instead of ten days later.

He never recovered from the heart attack; he drifted in and out of consciousness, was unaware of people in the hospital room with him, did not even seem to know where he was, and so after two days Anona returned to Whitney, to be with her children, the hospital assuring her they would phone if there was any change in his condition.

The phone call came eight days later, when Basil Sawyer looked not at all any more like the man who could once paddle his canoe from one end of the Muskoka lakes to the other. That morning the blood to the left artery of his heart stopped flowing. His body lifted clear from the hospital bed after the pulmonary shock. He came down, rolled off the bed and was dead before he hit the ground.

When Frank finished telling the story of Basil Sawyer and the princess pine, the mist had started clearing from the lake. Pine and spruce on the island across the strait were now visible, the lush green conifers stabbing through the remaining mist, framed by a sky that was cloudless and robin's egg blue. We ate our breakfast—bacon, eggs, pancakes smothered with maple syrup—then loaded the canoe with our trolling rods and a small pack of food. I pushed off the canoe, walking in the lake for a second, the water temperature warm and pleasant.

Once we had cleared a channel and started paddling down the east arm, the lake was almost ghostly. There were still thick patches of mist out on the lake, swirling around submerged trees and deadheads that appeared for all the world like the arms of drowning men. For a long time, as we made our way toward Park Side Bay, where we would fish for the day, neither of us spoke. The only sound was our paddles dipping into the water, and loons calling somewhere on the other side of the fog. It was only after we had cleared the watery forest, and the last of the mist had burned off, that I finally spoke.

"That was quite eerie," I said.

Frank just nodded.

"It's always like that on Ragged. The lumber companies flooded it years ago. Before I was born."

"Do you ever get used to it?"

"Not really."

Beads of perspiration were running down my back.

"When did you fish this lake last?"

"Last week," Frank said. "We were catching trout right off the shore. Cast out with a spinnin' rod, let it sink and the fish would hit 'bout twenty feet down."

"Did you use a weight?"

"No weight. You want it to sink slow. And flutter. That's what's natural."

Our paddles dipped and pulled through the water. Frank, in the stern steering with a J-stroke, seemed to take us perilously close to rocky shoals and submerged deadheads, but we never touched bottom. Within a few minutes I relaxed.

"What's your favourite lake to fish?"

"All depends. I like Pen and Big Porcupine. We'll go there before we leave. And Lavieille, I spent two summers there workin' for MNR [Ministry of Natural Resources] and I know that lake real good. All depends what you want."

"Do you have secret lakes you won't tell me about?"

"Oh yeah."

In the coming months I would try to get the names, and locations, of some of those "secret" lakes, but I never did. It was funny in a way. Frank would talk to me openly about his alcoholism and his love of Marie. Would tell me about his family, his childhood, his friends, his fights. Would think nothing of telling me stories that didn't portray him in a good light. But those lakes remained secret.

He even told me a story of a client he took fishing once, at one of those secret lakes, after the man had pestered him for years. But instead of taking the man directly into the lake, he had taken a wildly circuitous route that had more than doubled the trip. Sure enough, the man did try to find the lake on his own afterwards, but never did. When he came back the next summer to go fishing again with Frank, he spent their first day together cursing him.

After we had paddled for about forty minutes we pulled within sight of Park Side Bay. Frank told me to stop paddling and start fishing, warning me not to let out too much line.

"You want to be at twenty-five feet here," he said. "We'll be passin' over a shoal in a minute. Should get a strike there. We'll go down farther when we're out on the bay."

I put down my paddle and picked up a rod. We were fishing with Shimano trolling rods and Penn 203 reels. Frank has never used anything but a Penn reel, made since 1933 in Philadelphia, Pennsylvania. If you buy one, the packaging on the reel will tell you it's still a family-run business. The line we used was sixteen-gauge steel, made by Williams, although the company stopped making steel line years ago.

When Frank heard about his favourite fishing line being discontinued, he bought a case of it from a sporting goods store in Renfrew. Steel line doesn't tangle, or break, the way monofilament does and he can't understand why Williams stopped making it. I wonder if it has something to do with cost and shrinking market share, but don't mention it. No doubt Frank would find the reasoning silly. Fishing line is used to catch fish. The best should be available.

For lures we're using Williams Wablers, made for years by a gold refining company in Fort Erie, Ontario. The Williams family used to come to Algonquin park every summer to fish, and occasionally Frank used to guide Bud Williams, the grandson of the founder, although that job usually went to Walter Sawyer. Williams even switched his allegiance from Opeongo Lodge to Hay Lake Lodge when Walter Sawyer moved over there as a guide. The Wabler is one of your classic fishing lures, like a Mepps spinner or a red devil spoon. It has been used to catch lake trout in Algonquin park for seventy years.

I baited the lure with a piece of whitefish tail and started to let out line. One pass of the guide loop over the face of the reel equalled five feet of line. With the lure dropping at an angle equalling five feet of line for every one foot of depth in the water, I needed to let out 125 feet of line in order to fish twenty-five feet down. I counted the passes of the guide loop over the face of the reel, then threw on the catch.

I started to jerk the rod, the way Frank told me to, quick tugs straight up in the air, then let the line go slack until the lure gives a gentle pull. Wait two seconds and then do it again.

"It's all in the action." Frank will repeat that phrase many times. According to Frank, that's the most important element of fishing—not the bait, or the kind of lure, not even knowing the lake is as important as "action," the movement you create deep below the surface of the water. It is the one thing totally dependent on the person who is fishing, not on what that person buys or brings to a lake.

We cleared the shoal and started to troll across Park Side Bay, Frank telling me to drop the lure to forty feet. I let up the catch and watched the guide loop moving across the face of the reel. With the catch back on I jerked the rod again and look around, noticing a giant jack pine leaning over the water. If it were later in the season, and if the sun was hitting it properly, it might have been Tom Thomson's famous tree.

Although I didn't know it at the time, lake trout are caught most readily in April, May and early June, when the water temperature of most lakes is just above freezing and the fish are feeding hungrily near the surface— sometimes right on the surface—on flying nymphs and other insects. Starting in June, the fish go deeper and feed on insect larvae and the occasional foraging fish, such as small perch. By September, they are difficult to catch.

We fished Park Side Bay for the rest of the morning, but neither of us got so much as a strike. Shortly after noon we stopped on a nearby island for a lunch of Polish salami and cheddar cheese, Wonder bread and beef pepperettes, wintergreen tea and Fig Newtons. I asked Frank what we had been doing wrong that morning.

"Nothin'," he answered. "We doin' everything right."

"Fish aren't co-operating?"

"Right on."

After lunch we made several more trips across Park

Photo by Julie Oliver

Side Bay, but still nothing. Perhaps the lake trout had
scattered and gone to their spawning beds early. After all,
it had been a weird summer—too much rain, not enough
sun, maybe they were confused. Or maybe we were fishing the wrong depth, and not hitting "trout water," that
ribbon of water below the surface with the magical mix of
perfect temperature and ready food supply.

Then again, maybe we were just unlucky.

Finally, on one of our last passes over the rocky shoal where Frank had assured us we would catch fish, he got a strike. The tip of the rod bent like a bow as he started to reel in. Twenty feet from the boat we saw the first murky flash of the fish beneath the water, twisting and darting like a water bug. Although not big, it turned out to be a nice fish, six pounds at least.

Frank, who has caught tens of thousands of trout, was even more excited than I was. "My Gawd," he said, laughing and slapping his thigh, "that's a beautiful fish."

The Drinking Years

After cashing in his bus ticket to Timmins, Frank returned to Whitney and spent the rest of the summer fishing in Algonquin Provincial Park. He came out of the bush only to catch the bus to Cobalt and visit Marie. By the next year the couple had rented a house on Highway 60. Marie's five sons—Marcel, Guy, Joel, Armand and Michael—moved with her. Although the family's accommodation was spartan, things could have been worse. At least hydro power had come to Whitney in 1952.

Frank had begun guiding again, at the various lodges in, and near, Algonquin park—Opeongo Lodge, Hay Lake Lodge and Long Lake Lodge being his most frequent employers. Gordon Palbiski, who started Hay Lake Lodge in 1956, would claim years later that the two best guides he ever employed were Walter Sawyer and Frank. Sawyer was perhaps the slightly better fisherman, but

Photo courtesy of Frank Kuiack

Frank Kuiack (right) in 1957, at the age of twenty-three

Frank the harder worker. Once, Palbiski flew his Cub float plane into an interior lake deep in the Haliburton Highlands, outside the park, to drop off Frank, an axe and a saw. Frank had a hunting cabin built by the time Palbiski returned later that day to pick him up.

Like most guides, when he wasn't fishing, Frank had a variety of jobs. He did carpentry work around Whitney and built log homes for people in Ottawa; in the winter he worked for the Ontario government, doing road maintenance in Algonquin park. He also sold firewood, cedar hedges—anything that could be taken from the land and turned into money. And when there was no money, he would poach a deer out of season, or ice-fish illegally in Algonquin park (an activity banned since 1954), whatever it took to put food on the table for Marie and the boys.

It was guiding, though, that kept him busiest. Although most of the Sports had moved on, many still made the yearly pilgrimage to Algonquin park. There was Bud Williams, whose family owned the Williams Gold Refining Company of Fort Erie. There was A. J. Frieman, who owned the Frieman department store chain, headquartered in Ottawa. There was legendary trumpeter Al Hirt, a man so big he had to lie on his back in the canoe when fishing to avoid swamping it. Virtually the entire cast of *Bonanza*—Michael Landon, Don Blocker, Lorne Greene—came every summer. Greene even had a cottage on Canoe Lake.

113

Frank also worked at the Highland Inn, fulfilling a boyhood dream, although it was not what he had imagined. In 1956, the Ontario government purchased the Hotel Algonquin, Camp Minnesing, the Barclay Estate and the Highland Inn. The following year, all the buildings were dismantled and burned. Frank had a three-month contract with the Department of Lands and Forests, as cook for the demolition crew.

They brought the Highland Inn down in stages—first the boathouses, bandshell and the other outbuildings; then the two wings; finally the main building. They burned whatever lumber couldn't be salvaged on the shore of Cache Lake. In the end there was nothing left but a foundation line to show where the majestic inn had once stood. On the last day, Frank took a canoe out on Cache Lake and caught half a dozen lake trout for dinner. He battered the fish and fried them in butter, then seasoned them with pepper and savory, and served the fish with mashed potatoes and fresh corn he had talked a ranger out of at the park store ("Our last night here, boss").

Later the crew sat around the fire and passed around a jug of red wine, looking at the birch stand that used to be hidden by the inn. You could now see it clearly, the slender white trees lit up by moonlight. Most of the men laughed uproariously when, late that night, someone said, "It was 'bout time they left."

Frank didn't laugh. He just kept drinking until he passed out.

He awoke the next morning, stiff, sore, and with the now-certain knowledge that his boyhood dream of leading a fishing party from the Highland Inn was never going to happen. That morning he had the throbbing, discordant nausea of a hangover laced with more than the normal regret.

Frank had tried to cut back on his drinking when he first returned to Whitney with Marie and the children. He limited himself to red wine in the evening and the occasional shot of moonshine or brandy on the week-end, if the work around the house was done and some friends had dropped by. What could be the harm in that, drinking at home when the work was done?

Before long, the red wine was consumed in the after-noon, and not a lot of work had to be done to justify drinking moonshine. For most of those years—his heavy drinking years he would call them later—Frank saw nothing all that wrong with what he was doing. Hell, his dad had sold moonshine in the lumber camps for years. One of the last things Frank Kuiack Sr. ever did was give his son his still and customer list. (Years later, Frank would sell the still and customer list to a retiring police chief who was looking for a hobby.)

Almost all of the guides drank, and there were few social drinkers. In the fishing guide cabins at Hay Lake and Opeongo Lodge, where many of the guides lived during the summer, Frank would hold drinking

Highland Inn regatta, early 1920s

contests—with the Lavallys, the Parks brothers, Bill Currie—and he was always the one able to get up from the table and walk away. Lodge guests insisted on sharing drinks with their guides at the end of the day, and Frank could outdrink them as well. Hell, if he was going to lug a case of Scotch into the bush, he was going to have a drink when it was offered.

When he had no money, he drank moonshine from his father's still; when he had money he drank Scotch. If he polished off only one twenty-six-ounce bottle a day, he was exercising moderation. His diet, for much of his adult life, consisted of trout and alcohol.

There were problems from time to time—money problems, problems with Marie, problems with the children—but at least he knew what he was doing, not like those drunken fools who drank all day and then went out on Opeongo Lake and drowned. Once, he even won a canoe race when he was so drunk that when he woke up the next morning with the trophy cradled in his arms he couldn't remember how it got there. It had been a five-lake race, from Lake of Two Rivers to Galeairy Lake; and he won, people told him later, because he ran along the shores of Rock Lake carrying the canoe, instead of paddling it. Frank figured it would be quicker that way.

The race organizers didn't want to give him the trophy, but several people pointed out there was nothing in the rules that said you had to paddle your canoe, rather than portage it. Besides, Frank had out-paddled everyone when he was actually in the water. And the fact that he was stone-cold drunk made it heroic, somehow.

He was given the trophy, but told not to return next year.

There were many funny little drinking stories like that. Like the time he had been drinking with Bill Currie all morning, and the pair were so drunk by the time they arrived to take clients out for an afternoon picnic and fishing expedition that the family didn't want to get in the canoes with them. Currie assured them all guides

*Frank Kuiack with trout
caught by Hay Lake Lodge fishing party*

knew how to hold their liquor, and then fell out of the canoe in the middle of the lake.

"No problem," said Currie, splashing around. "Just checking the water temperature."

Or the time Al Hirt is alleged to have drunk three bottles of wine at supper and talked a guide into taking him out on Hay Lake, where he played the trumpet, lying on his back in the canoe and screaming to the loons, "Come here, you lousy birds, we'll have a contest!"

There were other, not so funny stories. Like the time Frank was pulled over in the park, so drunk that he couldn't remember getting behind the wheel or putting a loaded rifle on the back seat. He served two months in the Huntsville Jail for that one, although afterwards everyone had a good laugh about it.

"What wuz you going to do, Frankie? Kill yourself?"

He didn't think so. He had a dim memory of going after white-tailed deer. Marie asked him to quit drinking when he got out of jail, but he refused: guides who quit drinking were never the same again. Like Currie, whose doctors told him he would be dead in six months if he didn't stop. Currie was never much fun after that. His best friend, Mervin, quit drinking and then pestered him with invitations to AA meetings.

"Frankie, just come. It won't kill ya."

"Why would I want to do that?" Frank asked. "I don't have a drinking problem."

Marie moved into a separate bedroom but that didn't bother Frank. Just made it easier to drink.

By the mid-seventies, there were only a few fishing lodges left in the Algonquin Highlands—Hay Lake Lodge, Kearney Lodge, Livingstone Lake Lodge—all outside Algonquin park. Frank found himself working increasingly for the Ministry of Natural Resources, repairing roads and manning fire towers—as the guiding business faded away.

Algonquin park had changed drastically and fundamentally. The first autocamp in the park had opened on Lake of Two Rivers the year Highway 60 was completed. It was soon followed by other autocamps, on Tea Lake and Tea Lake Dam. By the time the highway was paved in the fifties, these campers were the park's most frequent visitors. They drove to their campsites, pitched their bulky canvas tents and lived there sometimes for weeks at a time. They cooked their own meals, took their children to the public beaches, went sightseeing with bulky metal cameras. Many of them never bothered to fish. From a sportsmen's paradise, Algonquin had become a summer vacation destination for young families from southern and eastern Ontario.

Frank would watch the visitors arrive in their station wagons and Jet Stream trailers, but rarely did he meet them. The autocamps had opened up the park to more people, but created a growing divide between visitors and the permanent population in Whitney. The new visitors had no need for outfitting provisions at the local general store; no opportunity to meet the people working at the park lodges; no reason to leave their campsite for anything more than ice, which could be purchased at a store in the park.

In those years, when he could, Frank took out clients

Courtesy of Algonquin Park Museum

Autocamp in the 1940s

who had been coming to Algonquin park for years. They were the last of the traditional "Sports," wealthy men from the United States and southern Ontario who now came to Algonquin for nostalgia as much as the fishing. After all, the fishing was much better farther north. You could fly into a lodge on Great Slave Lake, spend a week and be guaranteed of catching your limit while having a shot at catching a record-setting lake trout. You could no longer say the same about Opeongo Lake.

But some old-timers kept coming back every year. Frank would take out the elderly doctors and businessmen, assuring them it wasn't a problem for him to carry all the gear over the portage: take your time. We can rest along the way. He built spruce-bough beds for them at the campsite, and swapped stories of how good the fishing used to be and what a shame it was that the highway and the autocamps had ruined it all.

Frank was in his forties by then, but still one of the youngest guides working out of Whitney. There had been no generation following him into the trade. Those born after the Second World War barely recalled the Highland Inn and the Hotel Algonquin. Few even stayed in Whitney. It was a time of national prosperity, and good jobs were waiting in the car factories to the southwest, or in the federal government offices to the southeast. Who was going to stay in Whitney, paddling old men around a lake for fifteen dollars a day?

So the job was left to Frank and Walter Sawyer and Joe Lavally Jr. and Bill Currie and others like them. Most were second- or third-generation guides who had been taught the trade by their fathers. Only a few, Sawyer for one, still guided full-time during the spring and summer.

Frank fared better than most. Gordon Palbiski gave him steady work at Hay Lake Lodge. And Jan Van Ball, who had married Frank's sister Catherine, opened an outfitting company called Algonquin Canoe Routes. Those two men kept him guiding, while many others quit the business for lack of work.

Even the guide cabins were a thing of the past. Hay Lake had converted its guide cabin to a rental cottage in the early 1970s, and it had been the last one. At Long Lake Lodge, the guide cabins had been torn down and burned in the 1960s, to make way for the theme cottages at Bear Trail Inn Resort, the name the new owners had chosen for the lodge. They never used guides any more.

When Frank wasn't guiding or working for the Ministry of Natural Resources, he repaired cottages. Or did landscaping. Or sold cedar hedges to people around Barry's Bay. The cedar-hedge business wasn't all that different from picking princess pine in the forties and fifties: Frank would pick the cedar trees in burns and gullies in the highlands, then sell them at ten dollars apiece to cottagers. For another five dollars a tree, he would plant them as well.

Frank would describe his work as "catch as catch can." He thought that whoever coined the term had been brilliant. The perfect description of his life in those years.

In 1965 Frank's father died and, shortly afterwards, the farm on Mud Bay was sold. Like his mother's more than twenty years later, Frank's father's funeral was well attended. For his mother, there was standing room only in the Catholic church, and the police stopped traffic on Highway 60 for the funeral procession. For his father, the McRae sawmill was stopped for a minute of silence.

Frank got drunk early in the morning on the day of

his father's funeral, and stayed drunk for nearly a week. He had loved his father unconditionally, and with that lifelong need for attention and affection that often comes from having to compete with older siblings. Frank was overwhelmed by the respect most of the people in Whitney had for his father, as shown at his funeral. His father had been quiet and unassuming, a hard worker who rarely raised his voice, or boasted. Much different from his youngest son—except for the hard work—and Frank was aware of that. Always had been.

When he finally sobered up, Frank settled his father's affairs with his brothers and sisters. It was only then that the Kuiacks checked the survey on the family farm, purchased back in 1934. His sisters, Catherine, Mary and Bernadette, were upset by what they discovered; the boys, Frank, Edmund and Dominique, were more philosophical. This was, after all, the Algonquin Highlands, where ownership of land seems either absurd or pointless. There was plenty of land. And you couldn't build anything on any of it. Dad might even have been amused.

For it turned out the so-called hundred-acre farm was, according to the survey, just slightly more than nine acres. In forty years, no one had ever noticed.

One day you're sitting down to a drink; suddenly you're years older, and all you can really remember doing in

Frank Kuiack in front of Long Lake Lodge

those intervening years is sitting down to a drink. Hardcore drinking will do that to a person. And so the years passed quickly for Frank.

There was less and less guiding work—he noticed that. The park kept changing—more autocamps, more canoe-trippers, and now motors were banned on most of the lakes. That change came in the spring of 1979, briefly causing many guides and outfitters around Whitney to organize and petition the provincial government. It was, the group said in the letter to the minister of natural resources, the death knell for the guiding business. Without motors to get into the deep interior lakes, they would be limited to fishing on lakes by the highway. And who would pay to go fishing on one of those lakes, which hadn't produced a record-setting trout since the days before the Depression?

For a newspaper story on the protest, the Ottawa *Journal* sent a reporter and photographer to Whitney. The guides and outfitters posed for a photo in front of Galeairy Lake, where it empties into the Madawaska River. The photo today has the appearance of a historic relic, showing the last gathering of the Algonquin Highland guides and outfitters. Many of the men in the photo—Harvey Lavally, Paul Nicholas, Bernie Stubbs—retired from guiding that summer, when the ban went into effect. Algonquin park had been taken over by canoe-trippers. There was no place left for the sports fishermen. Why keep up the fight?

Frank kept on guiding, though. He liked motorboats as much as the other guides, but he didn't mind paddling a canoe around. He had done it his whole life. Could still do it easily. He hadn't slowed down, like some of the others.

As one of the last guides, Frank became well known to the conservation officers working in the park. Most didn't care for him, regarding him as a poacher and a drunk; but a new conservation officer, Jack Mihell, became a friend. Mihell was warned that befriending Frankie Kuiack was a bad career move, but he never heeded the advice. He saw something in Frank the other conservation officers had missed. Frank would bring Mihell fish, when he had some to spare and was driving by. Once, he brought him a bird he had hit on the highway. He had never seen a bird like it, and wondered if Mihell knew what it was called. He had a boyish curiosity about things like that.

Frank even helped build Mihell's house, on a hill overlooking Trout Lake, near Barry's Bay. Other conservation officers, friends from university, family from Ottawa—everyone who helped build that house came away with stories about Frank Kuiack. Like the way the man could walk up a ladder holding a four-by-eight sheet of drywall. Or the way he could make a finishing cut with a chainsaw. Or the way he could outwork any man on the site, even with a cigarette dangling from his mouth and a beer on the go.

Once, when they had constructed a subfloor and then realized they had forgotten to hang a plumbing line, the work crew sat down in shocked despair. The entire floor would have to be taken apart. Frank said nothing, but went to his truck, took out his shotgun, walked back to the group, and neatly blasted a hole where the plumbing line would go.

"Hang it there," he said, and returned the gun to the truck.

Frank was a little drunk at the time, but Mihell had to admit he had solved the problem nicely. Today it would be called thinking outside the box. Mihell wondered from time to time what Frank might be capable of doing if he ever quit drinking, and whether Frank ever thought about it. If he could work the way he did with a twenty-six-ounce bottle of Scotch in his belly, what could he do sober?

He wondered about that, and the reasons for Frank's drinking as much as he did, but Mihell was not a judgmental man. And if Frank wanted to drink, he was old enough to make his own decisions. All Mihell could do was wonder. And worry a little.

Marie said they had things to talk about. Frank had just returned from a fishing trip and had not even cleaned up. He said they would talk after he'd had his bath, but she said, "No, we need to talk now."

He sat at the kitchen table and rolled a cigarette. His hands were dirty and smelled of fish. It had been a good trip, with plenty of speckles and lakers caught on Lake Lavieille. They had caught their limit every day. The party had been a couple from Mississauga. Frank had been guiding them for years, ever since they used to stay at Long Lake Lodge. They had given him a fifty-dollar tip and told Frank, with a wink, not to spend it all at one place. He hadn't. He had gone to both the beer store and the liquor store.

There was money left over, too. Enough for groceries, and a little to put toward the rent. If Marie thought he had spent all the money on alcohol he would prove her wrong.

Marie sat down.

"Frank, I'm leaving."

He looked at her.

"What do you mean, you're leaving?"

"I'm moving back to Cobalt. A friend says I can stay with her. I'll be leaving in the morning."

Frank didn't say anything. He could feel himself getting angry, but knew that wasn't the thing to do. He needed to think for a minute, needed to figure out what was going on. He wished he could have a drink while he did his thinking, but that wasn't the thing to do either.

"Why," he finally asked, "are you leaving?"

"I can't live here any more, Frank. I just can't live with the drinking."

"Never bothered you before."

"It always bothered me, Frank. Maybe not so much at one time, but things are different now. All you do is drink. I never see you, and when I do see you you're drunk."

"I'm not drunk now."

"Not yet, Frank. How long do you think it will take?"

And Frank thought: to hell with her. If she's going to

accuse me of being drunk I may as well be drunk. He got up from his chair and went to the kitchen counter, where he had placed the paper bag with the Scotch bottles. He took out a bottle, unscrewed the cap and poured a drink. He took a sip, topped up the glass, opened a beer, then sat back at the table.

"What're you going to do in Cobalt?"

"I don't know, Frank. I'll figure it out when I get there."

"Not much of a plan."

"It's a better one than I had yesterday."

He was getting angry.

"Didn't realize it was so damn miserable living here."

"It wasn't always, Frank. Don't get me wrong. I still love you."

"You still love me?"

"Yes."

"So telling a man you're leaving him when he's just out of the bush is your idea of saying I love you?"

"When else do I see you, Frank? Getting out of the bush and having your bath is the only time you're here."

"That ain't true."

"It's true enough."

Frank was silent. True enough. What the hell is that supposed to mean? Something's either true or it isn't. True enough—that's just a damn lie. He kept drinking and thought about that. Marie sat straight in the kitchen chair, looking at him.

"So how are you leaving?"

"I'll be catching the bus tomorrow morning."

"What are you using for money?"

"My friend wired some while you were gone. I have enough."

"Enough for what? To get to Cobalt and live for a couple weeks? That ain't enough, Marie. Not damn near enough. You're not thinking it through."

Marie didn't answer. Frank went to the kitchen counter and poured another drink. It was mid-May and next weekend, if he wasn't guiding, he would be putting in the garden. He looked at the small patch of furrowed earth and wondered what he would plant. Then he returned to the table and sat down. For a long time they didn't say anything.

Finally, when the sun had fallen beneath the treeline and the light coming into the kitchen had grown flat and grey, Frank said, "Don't go."

Marie looked him straight in the eye. "I have to, Frank."

He didn't say another word the rest of the night. Just kept drinking, even after Marie began her packing, and the sun had disappeared. The light in the kitchen had gone from grey to filigreed shadows to dark.

The next morning Frank was gone before Marie was out of bed. He went fishing for a week, and when he returned she was gone. She did not leave a note, although Frank spent the first hour back in the house looking for one.

"Guess she said everything she wanted to say," he muttered. Later that day he began drinking, and there are some in Whitney who will tell you he never really stopped that summer. Frank swamped his canoe several times, and fought at the Whitney General Store, where people tended to congregate on the front porch in the evening. Gordon Palbiski took him aside one night and said if the drinking didn't slow down, Frank wasn't going to get any more fishing parties. Frank had laughed. "Who the hell do you think you're going to get to replace me?" Palbiski had answered, "Anyone who's sober."

To hell with Gordon Palbiski.

Frank never put in his garden. He wasn't eating much anyway. His days began with a beer, when he got out of bed, and ended with a highball and a cigarette before retiring. As he drank his mind started wandering, almost a continuous interior monologue, Frank asking himself questions like "where did I catch my biggest trout?" He would debate it for hours. Probably Lavieille, but he couldn't say for sure. "Who was the best guide I ever worked with?" He debated that one as well. "Is drinking as bad as everyone says?" "What's Marie doing right now?"

He developed theories on life and drinking that seemed brilliant one day and were forgotten the next.

Except for his three-drink theory. That he remembered and quite liked. Getting drunk was a three-step process, the coming together of three very different drinks. The first drink of the day was always bitter, something large and hot that moved down his throat and exploded in the pit of his stomach. There it would mix with bile, water and Scotch of the previous night. He would cough and light a cigarette. On a bad morning he would vomit.

The second drink was perhaps his favourite, not as harsh and overwhelming as the first, but still with a bit of a kick. His blood would start to warm. He would see things he had not noticed a moment ago. His muscles would loosen.

The third drink, though, was what you worked up to, the reason for the first two. This was the drink that changed things, that made a man large and powerful. After that you were on your way. Drunk again.

He never thought all that much, in those drunken interior monologues, about why he drank. If he had, he might have come up with the way drinking made him confident—that might have had something to do with it. He hated being doubtful or hesitant, and when he was drinking he was always decisive. The easy acceptance a drinking man has for another drinking man, that might have had something to do with it, too. There was something fraternal about drinking. A family waiting for you.

But he never thought all that much about the reasons

because ultimately drinking, like so many other things in life, just was. It existed. And how it came to be, well, that didn't matter all that much.

So Frank spent the summer of 1985 drinking, and taking a dwindling number of fishing parties to Algonquin park. He told people he didn't miss Marie, but moved out of their bedroom, and kept the room untouched. He tested his three-drink theory every morning. Frightened people at the general store. Passed out on his front lawn. Talked to himself. And in a thousand other interconnected and random ways, went more or less insane.

And then it ended. In the years since then, Frank has thought often about why it ended that day, and not another. If he had not quit drinking after going to jail, or after a drunken fight, or after one of the children begged him to stop—if he had not quit even after Marie had left—why that day?

He thought it had something to do with the fear of growing old and losing control. It was like being lost in the bush, or in the mines of Timmins when his miner's light went out.

He had started to drink early that day with his cousin. Homemade red wine at first, then rye, then brandy. As it was on most days back then, he was drinking for the cycle. The next morning he was awakened by a telephone. It seemed to ring a long time and far away, before he finally rolled off the couch and found the receiver.

"And how are you this morning?"

Frank didn't answer right away—he didn't recognize the voice. He was already ill, bile starting to rise, and he knew he was going to throw up if he didn't get a drink.

"Frankie, how are you?"

Gradually he recognized the voice as that of a friend from Barry's Bay.

"Fine," he answered. "Why?"

"You weren't in very good shape the last time I saw you."

"Whadja talking about?"

Frank hadn't seen the man in weeks.

"When you were here last night you were a mess."

"I didn't see ya last night."

"Well, it sure looked like you. And it sure looks like your truck parked in my driveway."

Frank put down the phone and threw up. He made a pot of coffee, his hands shaking so badly he spilled grounds on the kitchen counter, the floor, his slippers. He sat with his coffee on the front steps of his home. It was late September and the hardwood trees had already turned. The colours hurt his eyes.

He drank his coffee, went inside and picked up the phone. He dialled and let it ring a long time before he heard Mervin answer. He asked when the next AA meeting was. Mervin came over later that morning.

Fishing
PART III

When we returned to camp after our first day fishing we only had that one fish, caught at Park Side Bay. It was a disappointing day, but at least we had supper.

Frank built a fire and then went to the lake to clean the trout. I sat with him on the rocks, watching his filleting knife slice down the belly of the fish, then down the spine, then cross-cut so he ended up with fish and chip-sized chunks that he would batter, season and fry in oil over the fire.

"Could have been a better day," he said, without looking up. I wasn't sure if it was because of the work he was doing, or embarrassment.

"It wasn't a bad day. Would have been nice to catch more fish, but what can you do?"

"Not a damn thing."

Photo by Julie Oliver

It had been a good day. Out on the lake, sitting with Frank in the canoe, we had talked for hours. I soon understood why he liked trolling so much. Casting is a constant tossing and retrieving of the lure; fly fishing requires even more motion, along with such concentration and skill that it is best done alone. Trolling, though, is almost passive. You offer out a lure, paddle around a lake, and maybe you'll catch a fish. Go with a friend and you have a pleasant day even if you don't catch anything.

That day I began to get some sense of who Frank really was. He was shy. I hadn't noticed that before. He didn't look you in the eyes all that often, and tended to speak while doing something else—baiting a lure, paddling the canoe, starting a fire—anything that let him avoid eye contact.

He didn't start conversations all that often either, but was forthright and expansive in his answers. He didn't mind talking, just didn't want to do it all the time. He also spoke willingly on subjects that might have embarrassed others. Drinking, love for his wife. He told me, that first day, the story of how he met Marie, about their meal in the diner in Cobalt, and the decision to cash in his bus ticket and return to the highlands.

"Why did you do that?" I asked.

"I wasn't a miner. I needed to come back here. I knew that. And then when I met Marie, everything just seemed right about coming back."

"She didn't come back with you, though."

"I knew she'd come. I was going to court her."

"'Court her.' I haven't heard that in a long time."

"That's what we used to do, though. I came back home and started visiting Marie in Cobalt. I would bring her little gifts, things for the kids. I knew she'd come."

"What made you love her?"

"Everything. That's what love is, ain't it? I liked the way she looked, and the way she'd raised her kids, and the way she knew how to take care of herself. She liked fishin' too. I liked that about her as well."

"How important was that? That she liked fishing?"

"Couldn't 'magine living with someone that didn't like fishing."

Frank went on to say that Marie liked the taste of trout even more than he did. That woman could eat trout for breakfast, lunch and supper. She would have it with her wintergreen tea in the afternoon, and then again as a snack before bed. She would spread it on her toast, mix it in casseroles, bake it for Sunday supper.

"Never seen anyone quite as crazy about trout as Marie," said Frank with pride. When he said it, I remembered something he had said about another woman who loved fishing. I had seen it on a videotape, at Frank's home, the video of Ken and Wendy Chung, two long-time clients who visit Whitney from Mississauga every summer. Frank was invited to their wedding, an elaborate celebration with limousines and a black-tie dinner.

When it came time to toast the bride, every male in the restaurant stood in turn and said something. Many of the toasts were in Chinese; those in English were gushing and poetic. When it was Frank's turn you could see, in his pause, in the earnest and confused expression that played across his face, that he was thinking hard to come up with the nicest compliment he could. Finally, he raised his water glass and said:

"Wendy, you caught the nicest speckled trout I've ever seen."

Fish and love. Frank had been the only one to make the connection.

After cleaning the trout Frank walked up the hill to our campsite and started preparing supper. Before long, the fish was frying in the skillet and we were sitting before the fire. The sky had darkened, although it was not yet night-fall. In the twilight the sparks from the fire floated on what little wind there was, burning bright and then disappearing. Some sparks made it as far as the lake before turning into ash. By the time Frank had finished cooking the fish, the first of the evening's fireflies had appeared.

The trout was delicious—Frank served it with mashed potatoes and fresh cucumbers. To my own surprise, I ate three pieces. After supper he made a pot of coffee and we sat around the campfire, talking for nearly two hours. Stories told around a campfire used to be part of a guide's service, what the Sports paid for and expected. Frank had had decades of experience at this part of the job.

He talked about being in the bush for weeks on end, and about the time he stitched up an American tourist who had fallen down an abandoned log chute on Lake Lavieille, when he was working for the summer in a fire tower. At the Huntsville Hospital they thought a nurse must have done it.

He told stories about Bill Currie and Joe Lavally and George Phillips, a park superintendent and former fighter pilot who could land a float plane on lakes so small that no one else would attempt it. And he told the story, the last one of the night, of Jim Holly.

"Jim always liked this lake. It was one of his favourites," said Frank. "He caught the biggest laker I ever seen pulled out of Ragged. Twenty-eight pounds. Caught it at Archer Bay. He brought it home and had it mounted. I seen it in his study."

Frank went on to explain Holly was the son of the man who invented the Holly carburetor, and inherited a multi-million-dollar fortune. He invested it wisely—in Arby's restaurants and car washes—and became richer still. An avid sportsman who lived in Horseheads, New York, Holly came often to Algonquin park to fish. Frank met him one day in early May, when Holly was well on the way to drowning himself.

"I was coming out of a channel and I seen this canoe upside down," he said. "I didn't see him at first, because he was under water. Then he came up and, man, he was in trouble. If I had been five minutes later, he would have died."

Frank pulled Holly from the water, threw him across his back and walked three miles out of the bush before driving him to the nearest hospital. The two men became friends, and Frank was often invited down to Holly's home in New York.

Then, ten years after they first met, Holly suffered a stroke that left his jaw locked in a permanent grimace. Only after many months of speech therapy could he complete full sentences again, and even then his voice sounded like an electronically altered ransom demand. He started

143

to visit Algonquin park more often, its wilderness being one of the few places where he still felt comfortable.

Two years after his stroke, on the eve of his fiftieth birthday, Holly phoned Frank to arrange their fishing trip the following month. They talked for hours, Holly wanting to know what the fishing had been like that summer, and if Frank was still "reelin' 'em in."

The next morning Holly put the barrel of a hunting rifle in his mouth and pulled the trigger.

"He left behind a note sayin' he felt another stroke comin'," said Frank. "The note said he didn't want to live through that again. He was tired of people laughin' at him."

We sat for a long time after that, not talking, the obvious not needing to be said: out here, he never would have pulled that trigger.

The following morning I joined Frank by the fire. He was already drinking coffee. Not once was I able to get up before him. By the time we were through I began to wonder how much he slept. It must have been only a few hours a night.

"Ready for some breakfast?" he asked.

"Sure am."

And with that, he began to pull bags and plastic jars from his food pack. It was now the fourth time I had seen the food pack emptied, and I would argue you can tell a lot about a man by what he carries in his pack.

Everything about Frank is function. If Kevlar canoes, dehydrated food and Gore-Tex rain suits are the Holy Trinity of the modern canoe trip, Frank is the Antichrist.

In his food pack—the complete list—were the following: President's Choice pancake mix; butter, sugar and coffee, all in margarine containers; cooking oil in a plastic ginger-ale bottle; Smart Choice coffee whitener; McCain's mashed potatoes; salt; seasoning from a Mennonite farm near Bancroft; baking powder; tea bags; cornmeal; flour; Value Plus white bread; cucumbers; Polish salami; old cheddar cheese; Ritz crackers; Fig Newtons; brown eggs; and three moose steaks.

With the exception of the Fig Newtons, there was nothing that could be called a snack. The food was functional, purchased cheaply, and premised on catching fish. If we didn't catch fish that week, we'd be eating a lot of pancakes and salami.

There were no jars and cans in the food pack, nothing that had to be burned or buried or used only once and then packed out on the trip home. Years before "low-impact camping" became fashionable, Frank was doing it. In his drinking years, he even brought his moonshine into the bush in plastic jugs, to be refilled for the next trip. When Frank leaves a campsite there is nothing to show he was ever there. (He even sweeps pine needles over his tent site.)

The rationale of what to bring on a camping trip—only what works and has been proven necessary—also applied to what he carried in his camping pack: a ball of twine; the Eureka tent with the busted poles; an oil-stained canvas tarp; a nylon drop sheet; three pairs of wool socks; long underwear; a pink pillow; a 2½ pound axe; an air mattress; a Buck knife; two white T-shirts; one pair of green work pants; an old metal flashlight; waterproof matches; nylon string; a nylon rain jacket and pants; one four-litre aluminum pot; a percolator coffee pot, blackened and soot-stained; plastic plates, cups, knives, forks and spoons, two of each; a cloth skullcap; Irish Spring soap; bathroom tissue; one dishrag; a leather pouch of fishing lures; a roll of steel trolling line; a Crazy Creek chair; and a pair of Baycrest plaid slippers.

Some of these items Frank had owned for decades, like the tent and the axe. Some he had recently purchased. Take the Crazy Creek chair: easily transportable, and definitely more comfortable that sitting on a log or a rock. Plus, if you slipped the fold-up chair in the back of your pack, it gave a bit of extra padding on a long portage. It made sense, one of his few concessions to modern camping equipment.

Frank had tried clothing made with state-of-the-art synthetic material, but didn't think much of it. He said it didn't breathe properly, was ridiculously expensive and didn't perform any better than his old nylon rain gear. These things didn't make sense. It didn't make sense to bring a lantern ("I've got a fire") or spend a lot of money on a tent. Any tent, as long as it had a rain fly, was good enough for spring through fall. For winter camping, Frank never even bothered with a tent, preferring to dig a hole in the snow and build a shelter with spruce boughs.

He allows himself, besides the Crazy Creek chair, two luxury items. The first is the cloth skullcap, the lining from a pilot's helmet. Frank wears it to bed. He wears it in the morning, too, when he makes the fire, and it's a rather comical sight, Frank padding around in his Snoopy-versus-the-Red-Baron pilot's cap. But he says lots of heat is lost from your head, and what's the point in having a good sleeping bag and expensive tent if you're going to lie there like an idiot with nothing on your head?

The other item was a surprise, given the utility of everything else. Frank put his Baycrest slippers on every night after supper, and again in the morning; he didn't take them off until we were ready to go fishing. The slippers seemed so out of place in the wilderness—who in the world wears plaid slippers on a fishing trip?

Midway through the week, the obvious answer came to me: someone who is at home.

After breakfast we filled a Thermos with coffee. Before the mist had burned off the lake, we were on our way to Bonnechere, two lakes over. Frank wanted to be fishing when the mist cleared.

That morning the limbs sticking out of the water

looked even ghastlier than the previous day. They appeared suddenly out of the mist, their gnarled limbs almost scraping the sides of the canoe. It felt as though we were travelling through a battlefield. Had we found three old women on the shore, sitting before a campfire and telling stories of Scottish kings, it would have come as no great surprise.

That morning, you had to know your way down Ragged Lake or you would run your canoe onto a shoal or a deadhead. We were paddling almost blind, but Frank found every channel. Before long we were standing on the portage to Big Porcupine.

"This is a short one," Frank said. "Just follow my back so you don't get lost."

It was good advice. There was still a dense fog, and it would have been easy to lose the trail. I walked through the bush, following Frank's canoe as it cut through the fog. The mist whirled around my feet, and I couldn't see the ground, although I could tell by the soft crunch—there was no other sound in the forest—that it was dry pine needles.

At the end of the portage we put the canoe in the water and rested for a minute. It felt good to have already worked at that early hour of the morning. (Back in Ottawa I would have been sitting at a desk, drinking my third cup of coffee.) The mist was starting to break, and I could make out the channel on the far left, where we would cross over to Bonnechere. I was anxious to be on our way.

We paddled down the lake and through the channel, one more portage, and we were out on Bonnechere. As we paddled away from the portage, down a channel that had a sheer cliff on one side, Frank said, "You can go to twenty feet through here. Won't catch anything big, but sometimes you can catch them right through here. Over there"—and he pointed at some fallen spruce trees, half submerged in the water on the far side of the channel—"that's one of the best places in the park to catch speckles in the spring. On opening day, you'll catch your limit by lunchtime."

Frank paddled down the channel as I let out line, counting the passes of the metal guide loop over the face of the reel. He kept talking about speckle fishing, and how you could cast out toward those logs and catch a fish damn near every time. You'd have one of the best shore lunches of the season—nothing better-tasting than trout caught on opening day—on a rocky point we would go to that afternoon. Beautiful point. Perfect for a shore lunch.

For Frank, there is something almost holy about a shore lunch. By the end of the week, I was beginning to feel the same way. Not even supper, when the nicest fish of the day would be cooked, along with hearty side dishes—canned beans, mashed potatoes, onions, corn—tasted as good as the shore lunch. There was something simple and self-reliant about it. Fish all morning. Stop on shore for lunch. Cook the fish you just caught over an open fire. Eat them with cheese, fresh tomatoes and cucumbers, washed down with wintergreen tea. There is a ritual to it all—stop exactly at noon, build the fire, clean the fish, cut the vegetables, hunt for wintergreen, stretch out afterwards and sleep for half an hour—that Frank followed as strictly as a Japanese tea ceremony.

Shore lunches have always been part of the lure, and lore, of the Algonquin Highlands. The Highland Inn used to pack shore lunches for fishing parties the night before: the demand so high that the after-dinner kitchen was as busy as the day shift. Arowhon Pines continues the tradition today, letting guests order lunch the day before; the wicker baskets will be waiting for them after breakfast. It is like a picnic, with canoes and fish added. Not surprisingly, over the years many men from the highlands have used the shore lunch as a way of courting.

"Marie used to love her shore lunches," said Frank, after we had cleared the channel without getting a strike. "I'd cook up the trout while she gathered wintergreen. We'd eat on tin plates, off our knees. She never needed anything more than trout and tea, never cared if I had vegetables or cheese or anything else. Only woman I ever knowed who was like that."

"Does she like to fish?"

"Oh sure. She caught lunch for us plenty of times."

We were on Bonnechere now and the mist had cleared. The lake was a dark blue without a wave; no wind at all that morning. We quickly caught three lake trout, the biggest being about three pounds, off the point where we stopped for lunch. There was a tall white pine on the point and we fished in the shadow of the tree, then beached our canoe beneath it. After lunch I stretched out on a rock beside the canoe and fell asleep. A light breeze had picked up and I could hear birch leaves rustling high above me.

When Frank woke me up, I was surprised to discover it was nearly three o'clock.

"Thought I'd let you sleep," he said. On the way back to Ragged Lake he said I wasn't the first client to fall asleep after a shore lunch. People from the city did it all

Courtesy of Algonquin Park Museum

Shore lunch

the time. Quite often on the second day of the trip. Just like me.

"It's like you all show up tired," said Frank. "You just don't know it."

On the way back to camp I caught two more lake trout. We had supper.

Our days soon fell into a pattern. We would rise early and Frank would cook breakfast. We would then fish for the morning, on Ragged, Bonnechere or Big Porcupine. We would stop for a shore lunch, fish again in the afternoon, then return to camp for supper. The weather was spectacular, the soft maples turning crimson and gold. We paddled within feet of loons and mergansers and watched an otter swim beside the canoe. In the evening we sat around the fire and listened to barred owls.

We talked most evenings about fishing, Algonquin park, Whitney, or the guides that had come before Frank. Some of the more famous ones, from the heyday of sport fishing in the park, Frank had met as a boy. People like Chief Ranger Mark Robinson, a skilled fly fisherman who took out fishing parties when the park superintendent wanted to make sure fortune smiled upon them: visiting dignitaries, writers, politicians. Frank said Robinson knew his father and considered him a friend.

Of Basil Sawyer he said, "Sawyer used to scare me. He was a big man. You sure never wanted to make him angry." And he talked about the Parks brothers, Bert and Bill, who lived up on Paradise. You never saw them all winter, although in the spring, if you were out and about on the day the ice finally cleared, you would see them making their way to Opeongo Lake for the season. Joe Lavally—perhaps the most famous of all the guides—Frank remembered seeing around Whitney in the thirties, with a pet wolf trotting beside him.

"Never seen anything like that before or since," he

said. "I heard Joe had to shoot the animal one day, when it turned on him. You can't keep an animal like that as a pet. Joe was the only man who ever tried."

Lavally was featured in a book written by Bernard Wicksteed, an Englishman who went on a week-long trip with him shortly after the Second World War. Wicksteed had hired Lavally at the Highland Inn, and his book is a good account of how the guiding business worked back then. He had come to Algonquin after walking into the Canadian National Railways office at Grand Central Station in New York. There he picked up a brochure about "the Algonquin Park game reserve." Wicksteed quoted from the brochure in his book:

Game is abundant... bear and moose are occa-
sionally encountered. Beaver, mink, marten,
muskrats and practically all the fur-bearers are
fairly common... speckled trout run four to six
pounds and are best in the Petawawa-Oxtongue
River system... Lake trout up to 35 pounds are
caught in Opeongo and Smoke Lakes... Guides
are all old-timers with as much as 25 years expe-
rience in the Park and in bush life generally. They
know the best fishing grounds, when to fish them
and how, the best type of lures and tackle. They
know how to cook and make the camp comfort-
able and some of them are Indians.

The following night Wicksteed was a guest at the Highland Inn, asking for an Indian guide to take him on a fishing trip. He hired Joe Lavally at the Highland Inn's going rate of five dollars a day "plus subsistence," which meant you had to feed the guide. They cemented the deal with raspberry wine in Lavally's tent. (Like many guides, Lavally eschewed the guide cabin in favour of his own tent, pitched on the shore of Cache Lake.) The next day Wicksteed rented a canoe, camping equipment and fishing gear and purchased supplies from the store in the Highland Inn. They set out on their fishing trip the following day.

Much of the book is taken up with Wicksteed's never-ending amazement at seeing beavers, loons and bears and at being in a canoe with an "Indian guide." But it includes many details about what was expected of a guide in those years. After discovering their rented canoe had a small hole in the bottom, Lavally patched it "in less than five minutes" by heating up some balsam gum, mixing it with butter, and spreading it over the hole. He spoke of the importance of the wind in catching fish, and taught Wicksteed a rhyme well known in the highlands:

When the East Wind blows the fish won't bite;
South Wind they bite less;
West Wind blows the bait right into their mouth;
North Wind they bite best

Joe Lavally, standing, second from right

Lavally also explained that guiding was something he did not so much for the money, but to keep himself busy in the summer. His real income came from his traplines. It was there that Lavally earned what he called his "thousand-dollar cheques." Indeed, Wicksteed writes that the previous winter the Hudson's Bay Company was paying $110 for a single fisher pelt. That money made guiding almost a hobby.

It wasn't long before Wicksteed realized Lavally would make a fine subject for a short book. And a good thing, for in the autumn of 1945, just months after Wicksteed returned to England, Joe Lavally died, of unknown causes, in a cabin on his trapline. His brother Matt had been with him, and Matt carried Joe out on his shoulders to Whitney. He is buried in the town's Catholic cemetery.

"Joe might have been the best guide," said Frank. "I

never worked with him, but from what I've been told, and just from seeing the man, I think he might have been the best guide."

"Who else would be in the running?"

"Basil Sawyer. Bill Currie maybe. Oh, there were lots of good guides at one time."

"It must have been very different in the park back then."

"It was."

Frank threw another maple log on the fire and changed the subject to tomorrow's fishing. He'd been giving it some thought, and figured he knew how we might be able to catch "a good one" tomorrow. I let him talk, while I thought of the old guides, and what I had read and heard about them. I wondered if any one of them—Lavally, Sawyer, Robinson, even Tom Thomson —would have made a friendly wager on who would be the last of them. And whether anyone would have bet on a scrawny Polish kid named Frank Kuiack.

The next morning we headed back to Park Side Bay. It was there that we had caught the biggest fish of the trip, the six-pounder on our first day. We had since visited many of Frank's favourite spots on these lakes, and he figured it was time to return. Maybe that first fish had an older brother.

As we paddled I found him quieter than he had been on the other mornings. His responses to questions were short, sometimes only a word or a phrase: "right on," "okey-doke," "hard to say." He was looking around more as well, at the sun on the white pine on a far ridge, at the shadows moving across a nearby bay. Before long, his silence had become so noticeable it was worth a comment.

"Are you feeling all right, Frank?"

"Feel fine. Why?"

"You seem quiet this morning."

He didn't say anything for a minute. Just paddled and stared around at the hills ringing the lakes. Then he said:

"I'm going to miss this."

I nodded and didn't say anything. I wasn't sure what he meant, but took it to mean he was going to hate packing up and leaving in three days' time. I didn't think anything more about it, although Frank was quiet for most of the day. The fish were quiet too. We never got a bite.

A New Life

Frank went to his first Alcoholics Anonymous meeting three days after he quit drinking. Mervin Lagenskie sat with him during those days, making pots of coffee and talking about what lay ahead.

"It's different for everyone, Frank. Some people say they quit with no problems at all. Like snapping a finger. Others end up in the hospital. Don't know what it will be like for you."

"Never thought it would come to this."

"Nobody does, Frank."

"Always thought a man should be able to hold his liquor."

"There's no shame in it, Frank. I've been going to the meetings for nearly ten years. Wait till you meet some of the guys. You'll be surprised."

"Will I know them?"

"You'll know most of them."

It was unseasonably hot that autumn and Frank was sweating, even though he was wearing only an undershirt and boxers. Normally, he would have had fresh savory hanging in the screened-in porch where they sat, and the scent would have filled the room. This year, he never got his garden in. There was nothing in the room but the smell of sweat, stale coffee and musty bedsheets. He had taken to sleeping in the porch. Lagenskie was sleeping there as well.

"Just can't imagine not having a drink. It's going to be strange."

"You've already got a day under your belt. Think about that, not the days ahead."

"Is that what they teach you at those meetings?"

"One day at a time. Sure, that's part of it, Frank."

"What else do they teach you?"

"Why don't you wait and see, Frank?"

And so they sat, for two more days, drinking coffee and talking. Lagenskie was Frank's oldest friend—they had gone to school together, then to Timmins to work in the mines when they were both just teenagers. A lot of time over the years, although Frank never thought they'd be together like this.

There was something sad about having a childhood friend, thought Frank. It was good too, of course—no friends were better than the ones you'd kept since you were a boy. Yet he looked at Mervin and remembered how his friend looked when they were boys fishing on

Long Lake, a beefy kid with a dopey grin and poor luck. Frank used to tease him about it. And how he'd looked when they were working at the bush camp on Perieau Lake, back in the fifties—one of the biggest men in the camp although he was only a teenager. Now his friend looked older than his years: an old man sitting in his underwear, wiping sweat from his brow and wheezing when he tried to sleep.

It was the same for everyone. Frank looked at Mervin and reminded himself of that. Anyone over the age of four knew that. It was just that with Mervin, the proof of getting old was right there, staring at him. As much as he loved the man, he hated that part of their friendship.

Frank tried to read to pass the time, but couldn't concentrate. Newspaper stories blurred, all talking about people and places he had never seen and never would. He tried to read one of Marie's books, but it was a pulp romance about an oil sheik from Saudi Arabia, and he found the plot unbelievable. He gave up after four chapters. Television was worse. Every show made him restless and irritable, reminding him he'd rather be someplace else.

Mostly, he stared out the windows, noticing how the leaves on the hard maples had started to turn. And how the sky for the past two days had been filled with ponytail clouds, but it had yet to rain. And Long Lake, off in the distance. It was no longer called Long Lake because someone down in Toronto had decided there were too many Long Lakes in the province; now it was called Galeairy Lake. He wondered which Long Lake got to keep its name. Probably one close to Toronto. They would have done it that way.

Lagenskie watched his friend mope around the house. Although the AA cautions against it in those critical first days, he left him for an hour one afternoon to return home. There he picked up a small package and hurried back to Frank's house. He was relieved when he pulled into the driveway and saw Frank sitting on the porch.

"Here," he said. "I brought you something."

Frank opened the bag.

"You gave that to me when we were kids. Remember?"

Frank could feel tears welling in his eyes.

"I remember."

"At one time, that was your favourite book. I thought you might like to read it again."

Frank put down the Zane Grey paperback and started to cry.

The AA meeting in Whitney was held every Wednesday at the Anglican church. Mervin and Frank got dressed for the first time in three days, and Mervin drove them over. When they arrived there were already several men in the basement, drinking coffee and eating chocolate-chip cookies. Mervin introduced Frank to the other members, although he already knew most of them.

"How ya doin', Frank?"

"Doin' well, no complaints."

He poured himself a coffee and sat at the wooden table. Mervin was talking to a man in the corner, an old guide from Madawaska they both knew. The man laughed at something Mervin said and then slapped him on the back. Other men stood in twos or threes, talking and laughing. Everyone left Frank alone.

At seven o'clock the meeting started. The ten men sat around the table while one of them read a pledge, which they all recited back to him. There was some "administrative business" after that, the chairman of the meeting talking about a week-long "retreat" in Huntsville they could attend if they wished. The cost was three hundred dollars. After that he talked about news stories he had read that week. One concerned a well-known actor who had entered rehab, telling reporters he couldn't rationally explain his addictions or, as he put it, "I have no idea why I like the taste of cold metal in my mouth." The second reported that a new study in Britain contradicted an earlier study that had found two glasses of wine a day was healthy. And there had been a drinking-and-driving fatality in Bancroft over the weekend. He asked if anyone had any "business," or news stories, they wanted to discuss. They all shook their heads.

"All right then. Let's begin."

The man next to Frank spoke.

"Hello, my name is Jim and I'm an alcoholic."

"Hello, Jim," the men shouted back.

Then Jim started talking about his week, how there had been one bad day, when he fought with his wife and was sorely tempted to have a drink. He had been sober for ten years and was startled by how badly he wanted that drink. Didn't have it, though. All he wanted to say.

The next man talked of his job, and how his boss wouldn't give him any responsibility because of what he had done during his drinking years. But he had quit eighteen months ago, and when would he be treated differently? It was starting to make him angry.

The next man didn't think he was going to make it. Three months now without a drink and he was beginning to believe it wasn't worth it. If life was nothing more than thinking about something you couldn't have, what was the sense of it? Better to have what you want and pay the consequences. He thought this would be his last meeting. Just wanted to come and see everyone. The man at the head of the table said he wanted to talk to him after the meeting.

The next man was having problems with his children. The next wanted to drink again, if only for one reckless night, and what would be the harm in that? The next was more resolved than ever to stay on the wagon. His brother had just been charged with impaired driving.

Around the table it went, man after man talking

about doubts and victories and regrets. Frank knew many of the men, although he had never heard them talk like this. Frank stared around the room, at the fingerpaintings made by the day-care group held in the church basement three mornings a week. The map of Canada. The faded posters of Jesus.

Finally, after everyone had spoken, the man chairing the meeting turned to Lagenskie.

"Mervin, you've brought a friend tonight."

"Yes, this is Frank. He's my oldest and dearest friend."

The man nodded at Frank.

"Do you have anything you wish to say?"

Frank cleared his throat, thrust out his chest and said, "Hi, my name is Frank. And I'm an alcoholic."

Within two weeks of sobriety, Frank was surprised to discover he could breeze through portages that had left him breathless earlier in the year. He awoke without the drunk's bitter, copper taste in his mouth and more energy than he'd had since he was a boy. He phoned Marie in Cobalt. She was skeptical.

"You've been going to the meetings?"

"I'm going to my third one tonight."

"And you haven't been drinking?"

"Not a drop."

"No beer, no wine, nothing?"

"Not a thing."

They talked for an hour, although Marie said nothing about returning home. Frank never asked. He said he was guiding tomorrow, taking out a new client. He hadn't had a new client in years.

"He's a British guy. Staying down at Bear Trail Resort. I'm taking him out with his two sons." Marie wished him luck.

The next day Frank took the man and his sons bass fishing on Cache Lake. They could have filled the rowboat with fish. It was a warm day, with high clouds drifting slowly across the sky, the hills dotted with the sere colours of autumn leaves. The boys, eight and ten, were almost giddy with their success, once hooking fish at the same time, and so it became a race to see who could land the bass first. It was that sort of a day.

When they had caught their limit, Frank invited the family back to his home for a barbecue. The man had protested, saying he didn't want to put Frank out, but relented when Frank said it wouldn't be a problem, he could cook up a "fish fry" in less than an hour or his name wasn't Frank Kuiack.

The boys played in Frank's yard while he cooked the fish. What he didn't cook he cleaned, wrapped in butcher's paper and gave to the man when the family left. The man asked Frank for a business card. Frank said he didn't have any, but he was easy to find. The man smiled and shook his hand.

"I work for Shell Oil in London," he said. "I've been

fishing my whole life and I've never had a day like this."

"Come back again," said Frank.

"I think I will. I may send some friends over as well, if you don't mind."

"Don't mind at all."

That week Marie returned home. Frank turned fifty-three later that month. His decision—what he had given up, what he had accepted in return—seemed a good one.

The next few years were almost idyllic for Frank, the good years a man sometimes gets after a lifetime of getting things wrong. He was one of the lucky ones at the AA meetings, the one who quit drinking without much problem, the one who never had any doubts.

Before long Frank came early to the Wednesday-night meetings, to make the coffee for the men or, in winter, to sweep off the steps of the church. In the summer he would prop open a door, so the room would fill with the scent of spruce and balsam. After the meeting he would stack the chairs, lock up the church.

Marie was happier than she had been in years. The last of the children, Michael, had left home two years earlier and for the first time there were just the two of them. Many mornings Frank and Marie would take a rowboat onto Long Lake and fish, the mist breaking around them as the oars dipped and pulled and the fishing line whizzed with a high-pitched squeal when they got a strike. They would stop for a shore lunch, Marie gathering the wintergreen, Frank frying the fish on a grill he'd made of green maple branches. Afterwards they would fall asleep on dark moss, in the shadows of the forest.

Everything else in Frank's life seemed to improve at the same time. The client from London, a senior vice-president at Shell Oil, apparently did a lot of talking about his day fishing on Cache Lake. The next year people with British accents were phoning Frank at home. Invariably, they would be staying at Bear Trail Inn Resort and would start the conversation by saying, "David said we really should give you a ring while we were over."

They all wanted to catch bass, and were amazed at the fight put up by the fish. They roared like children on a roller coaster whenever they hooked anything above two pounds. At the fish fry afterwards—for the senior VP had spoken of that as well, and Frank did not want to disappoint the new clients—the men lamented the lack of bass in their native country. They were of the opinion England would be a far finer country with smallmouth bass in the northern lakes. It went well with ale.

Their presence was a sign that Algonquin park was changing again. From the American Sports, to the young families in the autocamps, the park had now evolved also into a popular destination for overseas travellers. People were arriving in the Algonquin Highlands from England,

Germany, Belgium, the Netherlands and Japan, all attracted by the park's rugged beauty, and its aura of almost quintessential Canadiana. The new visitors wanted to hear wolves. Canoe down a fast-moving river. Some wanted to catch Canadian fish as well.

Suddenly, Frank's guiding services were in demand again. Sometimes he couldn't understand what the clients were saying to him, as it was when he'd been a Polish-speaking boy, guiding the Americans around Long Lake. He would paddle the canoe, point to where they should fish and net the catch in silence. Then he would cook up a shore lunch and show the clients how to make a fire. How to clean a trout. How to make wintergreen tea. The new Sports couldn't have been happier, even though they didn't understand half of what Frank was saying.

The phone rang all summer long. Then the bus tours arrived, mostly Japanese tourists who had heard about the last guide of Algonquin and wanted to go fishing. They would pull into the Shell station in Whitney and ask for Frank by name. Once he took out sixteen of them for bass fishing on Cache Lake. Not one of them had ever been in a canoe. Frank had to give canoe lessons before he started fishing, but every person caught a fish.

He found he liked the Japanese tourists; and the Chinese customers from Toronto, who arrived at his doorstep that same summer, for reasons he never figured out. They all loved fish. They ate virtually every part of a trout, right down to the bones. During the shore lunch they would sit as a group, talking, laughing and eating the fish Frank had cleaned. His new clients refused to waste even a morsel of trout; he respected that.

It was strange how things had come around. When he started guiding it was a common vocation, something many men in the highlands did during the spring and summer, for customers who simply wanted to catch fish. Now there was a theme-park quality to it, as if Frank was an actor at the Canadian Pavilion. It was nostalgia that attracted many of the new clients, even if they had never experienced the thing they were missing.

Frank didn't mind the reasons for the new clients' coming to Algonquin. Nostalgia didn't bother him. He felt the same way some days. And as long as there were paying customers fishing in Algonquin park, it was hard to complain. Before long he purchased a house in Whitney, the first house he had ever owned. It needed work, but it had a good foundation, plenty of room for just Marie and him, and it came with a good-sized yard for his boats and vegetable garden. The house had been built on a small rise, on Maple Drive.

In 1993 Frank attended Algonquin Provincial Park's one hundredth anniversary party. Held at the opening of the new Visitors' Centre, he mingled that night with the superintendent, the scientists, the naturalists and the

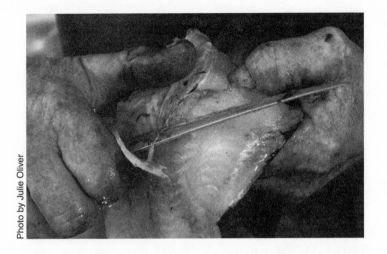

rich patrons from Toronto who had formed Friends of
Algonquin. He was given a belt buckle with the park
crest, and the years 1893–1993 on it. He put the buckle
on a thick, black work belt he wore every day.

"You look handsome, Frank," Marie said one day
shortly after the party, when he was on his way out the
door to take some Dutch tourists trout fishing. He had
blushed. Marie smiled, thinking to herself how, after all
these years, it was still rather easy to make him do that.

Those were among the best years of Frank's life, the
decade that followed his first AA meeting. When people
asked him if he ever missed drinking, Frank would
say, "Not for a minute. Just wish I'd quit twenty years
earlier."

171

He wondered from time to time what life would have been like if he had never drunk. But he was a practical man and never let the questioning turn to regret. There would have been no point. The drinking was in the past, and it was enough to have these good years. Frank figured that was as much as any man had the right to expect.

Still, it was a surprise when it ended. So suddenly. So unexpectedly.

For nearly four decades, the ten-year difference in age between him and Marie had never really been noticeable. Not to Frank, anyway. He had not even known her age until he was living back in Whitney and making regular trips to court her in Cobalt. It had been Marie who broached the subject, telling him how old she was, and then asking, "Doesn't that bother you, Frank?"

"Why would it bother me?"

"Well, it would bother some men. I just thought you might be happier with someone your own age."

"I'm happy with you. The day it bothers me, I'll let you know."

Age had never been discussed since. But almost overnight, it seemed Marie had turned frail. Suddenly she could no longer go fishing with Frank in Algonquin park. It was an effort to fish on Long Lake, and even then she could no longer have a shore lunch—it hurt to sit without a chair. She found herself tiring easily, sleeping late, leaving the household chores for her husband. Then in '97 she had a stroke and was hospitalized in Pembroke for nearly a month.

When she returned home Marie had good days and bad days, the good being when she could recognize Frank, the bad being when she would suddenly look around the kitchen and ask her husband where she was. She couldn't cook because she would forget to turn off the burner, couldn't shower because she would scald herself, couldn't go outside alone because she would get lost. Frank bathed her and cooked her meals and tucked her into bed in the evening.

One morning, a year after the stroke, Frank was leaving on a guiding trip and Marie's daughter was driving down from Cornwall to stay with her. Frank and Marie ate breakfast together and talked about the trip. Marie asked questions. She knew the lake and where Frank should be fishing at that time of year. She asked her husband to bring back a "good one." Frank felt giddy: he was going fishing and his wife was all right.

But when he was ready to go Marie wasn't in her chair by the window. She wasn't in the kitchen, nor downstairs. He found her in the backyard, sitting on a pile of logs. She looked at him without recognition.

"Can you help me?" she asked, as he knelt in front of her. "I'm not well."

When Adelle arrived he left with regret. When he returned a week later he drove Marie to a nursing home

Photo by Julie Oliver

in Pembroke. The day he admitted her was a bad one. Marie didn't recognize Frank. They drove in silence, Marie staring around the passing countryside like a child afraid of where she might be going. When the paperwork had been done, an orderly took Marie to her room. Frank followed. His wife would be sharing a room with a woman dying of cancer. The woman had been discharged from the hospital two months earlier and told there was nothing more that could be done for

174

her. When Marie and Frank entered the room the woman just turned on her side, to face the wall. The curtains were drawn on the windows, and there was an antiseptic-cleanser smell to the room.

Marie put her small suitcase on the bed and sat in a chair. Frank sat on the edge of the bed, his hat in his hand. His wife grabbed his hands and looked into his face:

"I'll get better here?"

"Yes," Frank lied.

He left the home and returned to Whitney, to live by himself for only the second time in his life.

Frank's guiding business had never been better. There was some comfort in that: in staying busy with steady work that put honest money in your pocket. Several of the new Sports became repeat clients. Like Ken and Wendy Chung from Mississauga. And Dr. Gow, a dentist from Brampton who wore a tweed vest and reminded Frank of Drs. Archibald and Stewart, the dentists who used to fish with Dr. McKenzie years ago. Dr. Gow never stopped talking, and called him Frankie just about every sentence: "Where are we going now, Frankie?"; "Going to catch lots of fish today, Frankie?" Frank had never seen Dr. Gow anything but extremely happy. The man loved fishing.

He made other new friends, too. Eddie Hovinga, the scientist in charge of fish stocking in Algonquin park, was briefly a neighbour. The younger man had been impressed by Frank's knowledge of the lakes in the park and they soon became fishing partners. Between them, they probably knew more "good spots" in the park than any other duo. Hino Rull, a local Ontario Provincial Police officer, also became a friend and fishing partner. As did most of the new clients. Frank's curiosity had never flagged. Many of his childhood friends knew no one but childhood friends. Frank pitied them.

He loved meeting new people, and learning new things. Taking a party of Mennonites bass fishing one day, he stumbled upon a seasoning he then started using for every shore lunch; he purchased it from their farm near Bancroft. From a party of Japanese tourists he discovered tiger balm, and used it every night before going to bed. The Chinese introduced him to a herbal drink he was convinced prevented the common cold.

The new friends, the work, being in Algonquin park every day, all helped to keep his mind off Marie. On one of his guiding trips he had been surprised to see, while looking at a map of the canoe routes in the park, that he had been on every named lake. He traced the map with his finger, from lake to lake, and started laughing. As a boy it was something he had dreamed about—fishing every lake in Algonquin park. And Frank had done it, without realizing it.

He brought Marie home as often as he could when he wasn't guiding, for holidays and extended stays in winter. But although he could portage an eighty-nine-pound canoe and a hundred-pound pack, looking after his wife exhausted him. He worried about getting old.

A year passed, then another. Marie moved from the home in Pembroke to one in Cornwall, where her daughter lived and could visit every day. Then she moved to a home in Notre-Dame du Nord, a First Nations reserve near the watershed of the Ottawa River, where she was born. Each move put her a little farther away from Frank. But he visited her every two weeks, booking his guiding trips around the visits. Notre-Dame du Nord was a six-hour drive away, and he stayed in a highway motel when he visited. On some of those visits, Marie didn't recognize him.

He would be glad to return to Algonquin park, taking the next fishing party as far into the interior of the park as he could. Sometimes he worked the clients too hard over the portages, but no one complained. And sitting before a campfire, with no other campers on the lake, helped keep thoughts of Marie from intruding.

But no matter how far he went, he had to return home, where he would be reminded of his wife every minute. He had even moved out of their bedroom, leaving it exactly the way she'd left it, so he wouldn't overrun the bedroom the way people do when they live alone. He kept the bed neatly made, the nightstands dusted, the floor vacuumed.

It helped a little. Just not enough.

He was fishing on Pen Lake when it came to him. Another of those rare moments of sudden clarity and certitude. It came with the strange brightness such moments had in the past. This time it was the way Pen Lake looked in mid-afternoon, the sun reflecting off the waves in a straight line to the far eastern shore. Frank did not have a poetic disposition, but even to him it looked like a path of light.

And suddenly he knew what to do. His mind calmed, the ceaseless questioning ended. He slept soundly that night, and for the next two days his fishing party, a couple from Holland, had spectacular success. The woman caught an eighteen-pound laker on their last day, as they fished their way down a channel that connected to Clydegale Lake. Back in Whitney he had cleaned the fish on the butcher table in his basement, then wrapped it in newspaper and waxed paper. The man said they were going to have the chef at Bear Trail cook the fish for their supper that night. They had eaten trout every day for nearly a week, yet they couldn't wait for supper. Frank wished the couple could become repeat customers, he had quite liked them, but he knew that Holland was too far for that.

After they left Frank washed down the table and went upstairs for his bath, thinking just as he had made their marriage work, and sobriety work, and his life itself work, he would make this work, too. You could think so much you got lost in the maze of possibilities, or you could just decide.

So he had decided to bring Marie home and make it work. As he sat in the bath that afternoon, scrubbing off the dirt and grime of the fishing trip, he made a mental checklist of what needed to be done. He would have to phone the home and tell them Marie was leaving. He would need to phone the children as well. It wouldn't hurt to have the house well stocked with groceries and supplies, so he wouldn't have to leave for a while, after Marie first got home. He would have to go to Bancroft sooner than planned, to purchase more Mennonite seasoning. He would have the Dakota serviced as well, while he was down there.

Frank got out of the bath and put on a pair of dark brown dress pants and a clean flannel shirt. He was going into town for supper. Giving himself a treat. As he walked around the living room, gathering his keys, his tobacco, his fedora with the feather in the band, he thought of what else needed to be done. Marie would need to start seeing a new doctor in Pembroke. He would need to arrange that before she came home. He would have to get the basement organized. He was installing minnow tanks next week, and he would do everything at the same time.

He would stop booking guiding trips. Frank almost laughed out loud when that thought hit him. Not once, unless he was already booked, had he ever turned down a guiding job. Who would have thought it? He was retiring. He might even tell some people down at the Algonquin Lunchbar that night.

Before leaving he looked at the calendar hanging next to the telephone on the wall. He had pencilled on it the names and dates of his future fishing parties. He flipped the pages of the calendar and saw it would be mid-September before he could bring Marie home. Plenty of time to get everything ready.

He looked to see who the last client would be. This time he did laugh. The reporter.

Fishing
PART IV

It was our second-last day of the trip when Frank finally told me the reason for his lengthening silence. We were fishing on Bonnechere, Frank paddling up the channel that connected to Big Porcupine, me sitting in the bow, jerking the rod every few seconds, fishing twenty-five feet down.

A few minutes before, a beaver had aggressively swum toward the canoe, as if to scare us away from his hut near the opening of the channel. He had slapped his tail on the water. Frank had responded by slapping his paddle. His was the much bigger slap and the beaver had dived, then surfaced far down the lake. Frank was still smiling, waiting to see if the game would continue:

"I'm sure going to miss this lake."

This time I caught it, Frank saying that he was going to miss some part of our trip.

"Why are you going to miss it?"

"This is my last overnight trip. If I'm just fishing for the day, this lake will be too far to come."

I didn't say anything right away, kept jerking my rod, waiting for a strike.

"Your last trip?"

"Yep, I'm packing it in when we get back."

He smiled. He had probably been waiting for the right moment to tell me. He had a love of the unexpected and the dramatic. The way he had met Marie and courted her, the way he had given up drinking— it was all drama. Now the time had come to give up guiding, and this latest decision was going to be dramatic, too.

"You didn't mention anything about this. What do you mean this is your last overnight trip?"

"I'm bringing Marie home. Going to take care of her."

"When?"

"Ten days after we get back."

I kept fishing.

"Got a couple day trips booked next week, and then that's it. I'll drive up to the home and get Marie. Already told 'em I was coming. They'll have all the papers ready. We'll come back that same day. It's 'bout a six-hour drive both ways."

"And then you're going to give up guiding?"

"The overnight trips, yeah. I'll need to be there for Marie. During the day, maybe I can get someone to come over, could do a few day trips next summer that way. I'll have to see how she is. But overnight, yeah, this is my last trip."

I got a strike just then and jerked the rod back. The hook was set fast, the fish still tugging on the line when I clumsily let it go slack a few times. When Frank netted the trout we saw it was about three pounds. We had our shore lunch.

The fishing for the rest of that day was disappointing—our shore-lunch trout was the only fish we caught. For supper that night we had baked beans, mashed potatoes and bread. Fig Newtons for dessert. Frank kept apologizing for the lack of fish. I had been the one fishing, but he was the one apologizing. Maybe it had always been that way for the Algonquin Highlands fishing guides. It was, after all, their responsibility to find fish for the Sports.

I had not stopped thinking all day about this being Frank's last trip. It was something I had not expected. But suddenly it was there, and a story that had been developing into a remembrance of another time and place was suddenly news, an era ending as definitively as our tents coming down in two days' time.

I needed to get the story right. The Algonquin Highlands. Frank Kuiack. Fishing. That night while sitting around the campfire I looked again at the silhouetted trees on the far shore, the ragged shapes of spruce and pine ringing a star-filled sky, and wondered if I would find the words to describe how this country looked, and how it felt to look at it. The peace and wonder of it.

Earlier that month I had read *Cactus Country*, written by American naturalist and author Edward Abbey. In his introduction to the Time-Warner book, which did not even have Abbey's name on the cover (some last-minute disagreement with the publisher), he wrote:

What I hope to evoke through words here is the way things feel on stormy desert afternoons, the exact shade of color in shadows on the warm rock, the brightness of October, the rust and silence and echoes of human history along dusty desert roads, the fragrance of burning mesquite, and a few other simple, ordinary, inexplicable things like that.

A "few other simple, ordinary, inexplicable things like that." Such a perfect description of the task at hand.

Would I get it right? The way a hardwood and evergreen forest blended, so you could walk on both pine needles and autumn leaves. Or the way you never saw a distant horizon in the highlands, for there was always a forested hill in front of you, or a lake that had to be crossed, or a river travelled. Unlike Abbey's deserts, this was a full, mysterious land, a place where people came

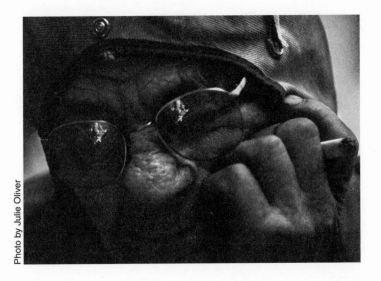

to hide—author Grey Owl, painter Tom Thomson—as though if you just travelled across the next lake, or over the next hill, you could disappear forever.

I looked across the fire at Frank sitting in his Crazy Creek chair, wearing his slippers, the flames reflecting off his glasses. He was smiling, not saying anything, and I knew I had to get that right as well. Why the man was here. And what it meant, his not returning.

The next day we woke early. Frank made a quick breakfast of bacon and eggs and we took our coffee in the canoe. We pushed off through a mist so thick it moistened our skin, and we paddled again around shadowy tree limbs and barely submerged deadheads. Once a flock of mergansers appeared out of the fog, swimming in a perfect line in the other direction, not more than eight feet from the canoe. Like us, they were silent.

We paddled for nearly an hour, until we reached Archer Bay, the farthest bay on the lake. There we stopped and poured fresh cups of coffee. The fog was starting to burn off, and I could just make out the nearby shoreline.

"Our last day fishing," I said.

"Yep," said Frank. "Let's hope it's a good one."

That morning Frank's silence disappeared. He was jovial and talked almost continuously as he paddled around the bay and then down the lake. Something had passed.

Frank talked about his career in politics for the first time. He was a councillor for the Township of South Algonquin. It had been a checkered career, losing once, winning once, getting the seat once when someone retired halfway through the term. He said he ran "just to annoy people that needed annoying." He tended to split the vote with whoever ran against him, usually a local business person. Half the town would vote for business, half for Frank. The elections were always decided by a handful of votes.

"If I was smart I would suck up a little bit more," Frank said. "That's probably the difference."

Coming from Ottawa, I told him that was exactly the difference. Elections are lost, every time, because somebody didn't suck up enough.

"Figured as much."

We caught two lake trout that morning, but neither was more than three pounds. The lack of big fish had started to bother Frank. He had been thinking about it for a few days now, why the big lakers seemed to be avoiding us. It could have been the summer—far too much rain, not enough sun, bitterly cold some evenings in July—maybe that was it. Although it hadn't thrown the fishing off until now. Frank had caught two ten-pounders in this lake just the week before.

"This is the first nice week we've had in two months, maybe that has something to do with it," he said after lunch.

"How's that?"

"Maybe they've 'climatized to the lousy weather. The sun on the water, maybe it's spooked them."

"They're a long ways down, though. How would they know?"

"Anything happens on a lake, they know about it. The naturalists will tell you why it happens, all I know is it does. The direction of the wind, the sun, what kinds of rocks are by the shore, it all makes a difference."

"All one big whole? You sound like an environmentalist, Frank."

"Don't know about that. Just know it makes a difference."

For the rest of that glorious, early autumn afternoon we debated possible reasons for the lack of big fish as we

paddled around Ragged Lake. It was the biggest problem we had all day.

"Come here," said Frank. "I'm goin' to show you a toy."

It was late afternoon and Frank was kneeling by the
shore, his Buck knife open in his right hand. We had
returned to camp early. The fishing that day—you could
now safely say it about the trip as well—was disappointing. Just those two fish caught in the morning.

"This here's balsam," he said, showing me a stick he
had in his other hand. "These here dimples on it, watch
what happens when you cut 'em open."

He took his Buck knife and slit open a small bump
on the stick. Sap squirted out and he put the stick in the
water. It moved like a water bug, darting over the surface
of the water and leaving what looked like an oil slick in
its wake.

"Sap from the balsam, mixes with water and
becomes a gas," said Frank. "When we were kids, we had
races with these. Get a big stick, with the right dimples,
it could scoot halfway 'cross the lake."

We sat by the shore and played stick boats for nearly
half an hour. I had noticed there was a boyish quality to
Frank. It showed in his shyness and his swagger, and
now, in these balsam boats. Although I did not know it at
the time, it would be a common trait among all the old-
time fishing guides I would find in the months to come.

Walter Sawyer, the son of Basil Sawyer, I would find

Photo by Julie Oliver

Walter Sawyer

in Whitney living in a converted garage next to his daughter's home. He said it was right across from the Howlin' Wolf restaurant, "which is closed now, but you can still make out the words on the building, where the stain hasn't faded."

Sawyer told me fishing story after fishing story, including how he got his first guiding job. He had canoed into Opeongo Lake with his brother Durland one spring—he was sixteen at the time, his brother one year older—and they talked Joe Avery into giving them

189

a fishing party. The next night, after the party had fished the far eastern arm of the lake and made camp for the night, Sawyer returned to the lodge. He found Joe Avery, as you could find him most summer nights, sitting in a chair on the verandah. Sawyer dropped a potato sack of lake trout by the old man's feet.

"Do we have the job?" he asked.

"You have the job," Avery answered.

The day I met him, Sawyer showed me the first photo I had seen of his father. Basil Sawyer stood by the shore of Opeongo Lake in a Stetson, sports coat and rough-cotton work pants, holding aloft a lake trout that looked to be well over thirty pounds. Sawyer still spoke of his father with almost boyish awe and pride: the old man could fish.

I tracked down Felix Luckasavitch as well, living in a nursing home in Ottawa. He was the second youngest of the fabled Luckasavitch brothers—Jack, Paul, Felix and Alex—giant Polish men who could outwork, out-canoe and out-fish almost anyone in the highlands. (Among the four of them, they also built the majority of the ranger cabins and lodge buildings still found in Algonquin park. Felix worked full-time for the park for nearly forty years.)

When I interviewed Luckasavitch he was eighty-nine. I told him I had just returned from a fishing trip with Frank Kuiack.

"Where did you and Frankie go?" he asked.

"Ragged Lake," I answered. "Bonnechere and Big Porcupine as well."

"Good fishing on Bonnechere. Go to the rocky point the other side of the channel. Catch fish there."

I smiled. That's exactly where we had gone.

I spent an hour sitting next to Luckasavitch on his single bed. Although the nurses had warned me that "you might lose him, his mind comes and goes," he told me story after story, just like Sawyer.

"You used to walk into Rock Lake, catch trout all day long. Didn't even need a boat. Then they built the highway and everyone was out there with you. Need a boat. Never the same after that."

He was raised on a working farm—not like Frankie, he said—couldn't guide all the time, had to help with the farm. But when he could, he'd guide. He was paid well: three dollars a day, back in the Depression that was "King's money."

Felix never liked pike or muskie—big, ugly fish. Like him, he said, and he laughed.

"What's your favourite fish then?" I asked.

"Ain't no fish but trout. Everythin' else is just bait."

I asked him about Frank. "Frankie was a good guide, one of the best when he wasn't drinking."

"He's quit drinking."

"Good for Frankie," said Luckasavitch. "I always kinda liked him. Just a kid, but he knew what he was doing."

Before I left I asked if he ever wished he were back

guiding in Algonquin park. It was a tough life; a lot of people gave it up and never had any regrets.

Luckasavitch looked around his room, at his pressboard furniture, his grey, industrial carpet, the two photographs of a long-ago family reunion tacked to an otherwise unadorned wall. Through his open window we heard the sounds of construction.

"Every day," he finally said.

Perhaps the best story of youth epitomized by the Algonquin fishing guide comes from author E. B. White. As Frank played with his balsam boats, almost hooting when one large stick sailed straight as an arrow for twenty yards, I was reminded of the story.

White once worked, and later partly owned, a boys' camp in Dorset, about twenty kilometres from where we were camped. Camp Otter was founded in 1910 by Cornell Professor Charles Van Patten Young. A former reserve player for the New York Yankees, Young was a fundamentalist Christian who always wore a suit and vest. He stumbled upon Dorset while motoring around the Muskokas in his new Packard automobile in 1909, a road trip that had begun in Ithaca, New York.

Young bought land on Otter Lake that year and opened the camp in 1910. Almost all the staff at Camp Otter had a connection to Cornell. White, a Cornell junior in 1920, fell in love with the camp his first season and returned in 1921 for a second summer. Seven years later, by then a mainstay at *The New Yorker*, White returned to

Camp Otter, first as a counsellor, then as a part-owner, having bought shares from his brother-in-law.

Quitting *The New Yorker*, leaving the city, talking of quitting writing was the sort of thing White would do throughout his life. He always doubted himself as a writer, an uncertainty that manifested itself in mood swings, ill health and many stops and starts in his career. He had a "hankering for a vague but majestic magnum opus," John Updike once said of his close friend.

In the end, that masterpiece was *Charlotte's Web*, a fanciful tale regarded by many as the finest children's story ever written. White wrote two other children's books as well, *Stuart Little*, published in 1945, seven years before *Charlotte's Web*, and *The Trumpet of the Swan*, published when he was seventy-one.

This last book is an homage to the Algonquin Highlands. There is a chapter called Camp Kookooskoos, which describes Camp Otter right down to its extended wharf and dive tower. The scenery in the book is all highlands. As are many of the characters.

I knew about White's years in Dorset because I had written a story on Camp Otter a year earlier. I had found the old camp, even tracked down Olga Cunningham, whose father used to be the caretaker.

I will never forget flipping through her photo albums, and Cunningham stopping at a photo of a tall man with a large, white moustache. He was sitting in front of a log cabin, beside a fine string of speckled trout

Photo courtesy of Olga Cunningham

E. B. White at Camp Otter in the 1920s

strung across the porch. Cunningham told me his name.

And there was Sam Beaver. It turned out that White, working far away on his farm in Maine, with an ailing wife, with failing health himself, with almost certain knowledge this would be one of his final books, chose to write a children's book about the Algonquin Highlands. And named his boy protagonist after a fishing guide in Dorset.

After another supper of mashed potatoes and baked beans while sitting around the campfire, I thought again about Edward Abbey's exhortations, and wondered how I would describe Frank Kuiack.

The physical description would pose no problem: five foot six, 156 pounds, sixty-six years old. A bald spot on the back of his head usually hidden by a ball cap. A ring of short hair around the bald spot. Face wrinkled and weathered. Small mouth. Large ears. Cocky way of walking. Clears his mouth before speaking. Rarely looks you in the eye.

I could describe obvious personality traits as well. He was shy and compensated for it with a blustery manner. He was frugal almost to the point of stinginess. He had a good sense of humour. He was earnest. Hard-working. Sentimental. Emotions played readily across his wrinkled face. And he was boyish.

He wouldn't like that bit, but it helped to answer why Frank Kuiack, of all the thousands who went before

Sam Beaver (far right)

him, ended up being the last of the Algonquin Highland fishing guides. Whoever was last would have to have a childlike quality. Absolutely needed to.

This was not a job you did for money, or advancement or any of the other reasons adults normally work. To do this job, especially when the world around you had "grown up," you needed other motivation. A love of fishing, obviously. A love of an uncomplicated life. A love of doing something well, and people noticing. You needed to guide for the reasons a small boy wants to impress his father: so the world would make sense and offer some measure of comfort and affirmation.

But most guides had this quality, not just Frank. So, was Frank's being the last guide nothing more than simple attrition? Someone had to be last, why not Frank? I had wondered about that, but in the end discarded such an argument. There had to be a logic to what had happened.

Those thoughts were running through my head on that last night, as we sat around the campfire telling stories. Frank didn't seem to want to go to bed. He made three pots of coffee. Finished off the Fig Newtons. Went out near midnight with a glass jar to catch fireflies. I tried to catch the insects with my hands, the way Frank was doing it. I dove on them whenever they appeared, but missed every time. If you had been on a campsite across the channel, you would have heard our laughter. After Frank caught half a dozen fireflies, and both of us looked in wonder at the iridescent insects in the jar, we let them go and returned to the campfire.

It was then that I decided to just ask the question.

"Frank, why do you still guide?"

"What do you mean?"

"Well, I've been wondering about it. Everyone else has given it up. Nobody else thinks it's worthwhile any more. Why do you bother?"

"Maybe I never really had the chance to quit. The clients never went away. Long as they kept phoning me and asking to go fishing, I didn't see the sense in staying home."

"Is that the only reason?"

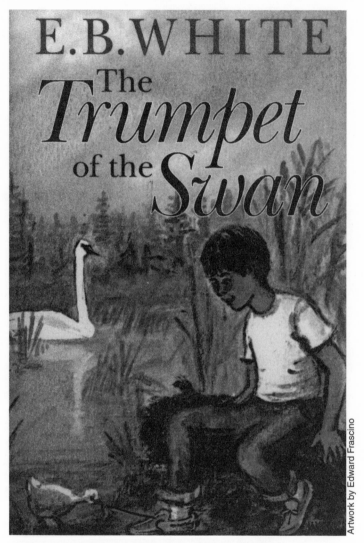

Trumpet of the Swan, *E. B. White's*
last children's book

"It's a good one, don't you think?"

"Not bad. But you're not answering the question. Is that the only reason?"

He stared at the campfire and shrugged, a mannerism I had come to know well. Next, he would look for something to do, maybe grab another log and put it on the fire, so he could fuss with his hands for a minute and not look at me. Then he would clear his throat. Then he would speak.

And after he had done all that, he said, "You remember that story of Jim Holly I was telling you about."

"Sure."

"Well, that always stayed with me. It seemed to me Jim was most happy out here in the woods. Yet he lived someplace else. I think that's what the problem was. He wasn't doing what he wanted, and I got to thinking about it, and maybe I decided I shouldn't make that same mistake."

"You think that's why he killed himself?"

"No," said Frank, "he was already killing himself. He just used the shotgun to finish the job."

That night, all the stories I had read about the Algonquin Highlands and the old-time fishing guides seemed to mesh into one long, rambling dream. I saw Joe Lavally walking down a trail with a pet wolf trotting beside him; and Basil Sawyer, counting bags of princess pine in a railway yard in North Bay. I was there for Tom Thomson's last fishing trip, and thought, for a moment, I knew what happened; but then other faces came in and out of focus: Mark Robinson, Bill Currie, E. B. White; I saw myself picking up a shore lunch at the Highland Inn, then walking to the boathouse to meet the guide. Saw fast-moving rivers and trout circling in a cool, dark pool on the far shore. Saw the unknown British family Mark Robinson found at the turn of the last century, homesteading on Dickson Lake, miles from any portage route: a mother, father and two beautiful teenage daughters, living in a log cabin with a piano in the parlour.

How in the world did they get the piano there? How in the world... and then Grey Owl was snowshoeing across a frozen lake, laughing at the park rangers who were trying to stop him. The last train pulled into Cache Lake station; a big-finned fifties station wagon pulled into an autocamp; Walter Sawyer was laughing and filling a potato sack with trout; I was sitting in a strange kitchen, looking at stuffed fish and drinking coffee, while a small, wrinkle-faced man talked about wolves.

The next morning I woke feeling tired, and stayed in my tent for a long time. We would not fish that day, just break camp, head back to the Smoke Lake dock, then down Highway 60 and out of Algonquin park. We would drop off the gear at Frank's house, then I would head back to Ottawa. That night I would be home, sleeping in my own bed.

I stayed in the sleeping bag for what seemed the better part of the morning, although even in my half-asleep state I knew that couldn't be the case. We had been getting up early during the trip—some mornings I had seen the sun clear the treeline—and when I finally did unzip my sleeping bag and looked at my watch, it was 6:45.

I pulled on a sweater—the mornings seemed to have gotten colder even in the week we had been here—and opened the flap of my tent. Frank was sitting by the campfire. I had found him every morning sitting in his Crazy Creek chair, poking at the embers in the fire with a maple branch.

I pulled on my boots and walked down to the fire.

"Coffee's on."

"I knew that," I said. "Coffee's on every morning."

"Right on."

We sat there for a minute, drinking our coffee and looking at the fire.

"What would you like for breakfast?" he asked.

"I don't know. How about bacon, eggs and pancakes? Do we have that?" With the exception of trout, which we didn't have, it was the breakfast we had had every morning of the trip.

"I think we have that," he answered. Frank kept poking at the embers in the fire, the tip of the maple branch glowing like the cigarette in his mouth. Finally he put the stick down, walked to the food pack and started pulling out plastic containers and packages wrapped in butcher's paper. I watched as he put bacon in one of the aluminum fry pans and placed it on the middle of the grill, the flames from the fire licking the sides of the pan.

Using his hands he moved the bacon strips around the frying pan, eventually placing the cooked meat on a sheet of newspaper on the ground. While he did that he mixed the pancakes, adding a pinch of baking soda, which he had told me was the secret to making a good pancake. Companies didn't put enough baking soda in their instant pancake these days. He poured the batter into another frying pan.

When all the bacon was cooked he cracked two eggs on the side of the pan and cooked them in the bacon grease, the edges curled and singed, and placed them on a plastic plate. He placed six pieces of bacon next to the eggs, then slid out the pancakes. I smothered everything with maple syrup.

"I'm going to miss these breakfasts, Frank."

He nodded, but didn't say anything.

After breakfast I started packing up my tent. I rolled up the sleeping bag, packed my clothes, pulled apart the poles. In a minute the tent was on the ground, waiting to be rolled up and packed away. For the first time, I seemed to be ahead of Frank, who was taking his time cleaning the dishes and loading the Woods rucksacks. His Eureka tent was still set up on the rise above me.

I stopped working and sat down. I was in no hurry and it was going to be another glorious day, once the morning chill had burned off. I looked across the chan-

Mergansers

nel at the island facing our campsite, and noticed more of the maples had turned.

Slowly I packed up my tent, while Frank walked up the hill to do the same. The Woods rucksacks were packed and waiting by the canoe. Frank brushed pine needles over the spot where his tent had been, then doused the fire with water and neatly stacked our unused wood under a tall red pine for the next campers. Then we loaded the canoe and pushed off from shore.

We paddled with the sun in our eyes, the day already hot out on the lake. Mergansers swam beside us. We saw an otter scamper down a rock and then slide into the water with a splash. When we got to the portage Frank again hoisted the canoe on his shoulders and headed down the trail without waiting for me. I carried one of the Woods packs and left the other for him.

We put the canoe back in the water and started to make our way to the boat launch on Smoke Lake. I was surprised when Frank stopped paddling a few times,

resting the paddle across his knee and staring around at the shoreline. He had not done that once during our trip. I took off my T-shirt and started to stroke heavily in the water, enjoying the sweat trickling down my back and wondering when I would next be back out on a lake. I was already missing it.

At the boat launch we tied up and Frank went to get his truck. We loaded the canoe into the bed of the truck, threw in the gear and tied down the canoe with rope. Next to us a family from Toronto were unloading two Scott Kevlar canoes and their gear, most of it stored in bright-blue water barrels. Frank stood for a minute, staring down the lake at where the sun was hitting a clump of tall pine, and where he knew the portage was to Ragged Lake. He just stood there, tossing his truck keys in his hand. Finally he turned around and said, "Come on, let's go."

Epilogue:
The Last Guide

Ten days after our fishing trip Frank discharged Marie from the Anishnabe Long-Term Care Centre on the Timiskaming First Nations Reserve. Back home Marie had good days, and some bad days when she would sit at the kitchen table and suddenly look around the room, wondering where she was. Frank hired a live-in house-keeper, a Cuban woman who had fallen in love with a man in Peterborough. Frank sponsored the woman's immigration, although mostly as a favour for the man in Peterborough. A good cook and housekeeper, the woman stayed until early spring, when she left to get married.

That autumn, after trout season ended in the park, Frank spent most of his days fishing on Raglan Lake, catching whitefish that he would can for winter. On some days he fished with Hino Rull or Eddie Hovinga, occasionally with some men from Whitney, although on most days he fished alone, from a 1943 Peterborough, his favourite fishing boat.

Frank didn't run to keep his seat on the South Algonquin council that fall. He had begun to think of politics as a thankless occupation, and had to admit he had no great understanding of it. The relocation of the Whitney town office the year before, to Madawaska, which was more central in the new amalgamated township, had made perfect sense to Frank—you just had to look at a map. But his vote in favour of the move was seen by many in Whitney as a betrayal. That surprised him, and left him feeling uncertain of his actions. He quit politics without regret. On Thanksgiving Sunday the story about Frank appeared in the *Citizen*'s weekly magazine and Frank was teased around Whitney that he must still be running for office.

Hunting season came and went but Frank didn't get a moose tag in the lottery that year, and the deer season was disappointing. He got a small buck, on a crisp November morning, down by Raglan Lake. The deer fell cleanly in a clearing covered with dead autumn leaves and hoar frost, and that was the only deer that year. Shortly after hunting season I phoned to say a publisher wanted to publish the story of his life and last fishing trip. I can't stay away, I joked, and told him I would be up to see him after Christmas.

Frank purchased a semi-trailerload of maple and birch from a woodlot dealer in Bancroft that fall, and when not fishing on Raglan he was chopping wood, which he sold around Whitney for forty-five dollars a face cord. He had a splitter, but rarely used it—it was quicker to chop by hand. The late-autumn days that year were warm and he enjoyed working outside until late November, when a heavy rain stripped the last of the leaves from the birch trees. Overnight the rain turned to snow and winter had returned.

That year it snowed more than it had in decades, once for fifteen straight days in the Algonquin Highlands. The snow fell in thick, moist flakes most days, that a strong wind swirled around before they finally landed. In those weeks, what could be seen of the day sky was a light, washed-out grey. There was no horizon, or sense of distance, and when walking outside you fast became light-headed and felt slightly off balance. Those who could, stayed inside and slept.

On the tenth day of the storm, in what was perceived at the time as a miraculous occurrence, the snow stopped falling. People in Whitney awoke that day to discover the sky had turned the colour of faded denim. The sun was visible again. The snow on the ground was bright and radiant, hard to look at, although people walked around looking at it anyway and shielding their eyes.

On that morning I awoke in a small room in the East

Gate Motel, on Highway 60, and like everyone else was surprised to see how the world had changed. I dressed in warm clothes and headed toward Frank's house.

That morning Frank got out of bed, dressed in long underwear and dark-green work clothes, put on his Buckmasters ball cap and went downstairs to the kitchen. Marie was already sitting in her chair by the window.

"Morning, Frank," she said.

"Mornin' Mother."

He put on a pot of coffee, and a kettle of water for Marie's wintergreen tea, then sat at the kitchen table and rolled a cigarette. The housekeeper was still asleep and he didn't bother waking her. He made his coffee, and slipped two pieces of white bread into the toaster. He got a plastic container of boiled trout from the fridge and when the toast popped up he spread some of the fish on it. Then he made Marie's tea and brought the breakfast to her on a television-dinner tray. He sat beside her, smoking his cigarette, and stared out the window.

"Look how high the snow is up the tree, Frank," said Marie. "I don't think I've ever seen it so high." Frank nodded and said nothing, although he thought there might have been a few years with more snow. That second winter in the lumber camp, on Perieau Lake, he thought there might have been more snow then. And the long winter his father died, with the freak spring storm at the end of it, the day of the funeral. Still, there was a lot of snow, no doubting that.

"Do you want me to turn on the television?" he asked, after a few minutes.

"That would be nice."

Frank got up from his chair, found the television remote on the table and turned on the television. That autumn Marie's doctor had told her to stop watching television, something to do with the need to protect her weak eyes, and so she had stopped, even though she used to enjoy watching game shows, and soap operas, and old sitcoms on the Comedy Channel. Frank flipped to an episode of *All in the Family*, put down the remote and returned to his seat. Marie laughed at the jokes and only occasionally had to ask Frank what was happening.

"What does the fellow look like, Frank?"

"He's a big man, looks like he works in a factory."

"And what's Edith doing?"

"She's still in the kitchen."

Marie kept staring out the window, laughing at the jokes on the television, wondering, as she told me later, if the doctor was right about her eyes. He was a new doctor. Awfully young.

Frank cleared the dishes and then went outside to start chopping wood. Tom Sawyer, Neil's boy, had been phoning the past two days, asking for three more cords. The other day, someone had told him it was Neil's dad who had invented the Williams Wabler. Basil Sawyer had

Marie and Frank

been out fishing with Bud Williams on Opeongo Lake
one day and Bud had brought a new lure. He showed it
to Basil, and Basil said it would never work, you needed
to put a twist in it so it would flutter in the water. Then
he took out a pair of pliers and bent the lure right in
front of Bud, who caught five lake trout in a row right
afterwards. Frank wondered if the story was true. Might
have been. Sounded like Basil.

Sounded the way things work a lot of times, too.
Williams probably had people working for him who had

spent months inventing that lure, never knowing you needed a twist in it. When he thought about it for any length of time, Frank had to admit he had rarely seen a man's plans work out. Show him the man living the life he planned, he'd never met him.

The previous night he had attended his weekly AA meeting at the Anglican church—and what better argument for the folly of plans did you need? What man plans on becoming an alcoholic? Because of the snow it had been a small meeting, just half a dozen men. Some of the newer members—their eyes looking around the room, their weight shifting in the fold-out chairs—you could just tell their plans were falling apart. The men had Frank's phone number, and he would be surprised if he didn't receive a desperate late-night phone call in the next few weeks.

Rejean, the only member who had been sober longer than Frank, told the meeting he had been to the hospital in Ottawa earlier in the week, trying to clear out the arteries to his heart, using balloons that didn't work. After sixteen hours he was sent home and told he'd be put on a waiting list for a bypass operation. He was older than Frank, smoked more than Frank and was pretty sure his name was well down that list. He made jokes about it at the meeting, but at least there was a man with a plan that made sense: stay alive.

Frank told me all this later in the day. When I first saw him that morning he was chopping wood, silent and so intent on the job I was nearly upon him before he saw me.

"Coffee's on," he said, and I went inside.

I walked past the fishing tackle, the minnow tanks, the Folgers coffee cans and muddy hip waders, and climbed the stairs. It seemed a long time ago that I had first entered this home. None of it surprised me as it once had: not the clutter on the stairs; or the boats in the yard; or the boy's bedroom tucked away behind a partition wall in the basement, where a sixty-six-year-old man still slept on occasion, in a sleeping bag surrounded by fishing lures and maps of Algonquin park. This was where Frank went on nights when he had trouble sleeping on sheets and feather pillows, when he would leave his wife alone in bed, so he could smoke cigarettes downstairs and wait for the deep-sleep dreams of his youth.

At the top of the stairs I looked around at the stuffed fish on the walls, the *Thank You For Not Smoking* sign, the ashtray on the kitchen table, and none of that surprised me either. Marie was sitting in a chair by a window in the living room, drinking tea, and I said hello.

"It's quite the morning," she said.

"It's unbelievable," I answered. "I can't recall a storm ever clearing like this before."

I poured myself a coffee and sat in Frank's chair next to the window. Marie told me a new grandchild had been born that past autumn to her son Armand, who lived in Cornwall with his second wife. Grandchild number nineteen. He'd come for Christmas, already crawling and for sure he would be a big boy. Might even be walking come spring.

She said it felt good to be home. She never cared for nursing homes, never found one any better than the last. At Anishnabe she thought it would be better—she had family on the reserve—but she quickly realized it had been a long time since she last lived there. Cousins came to visit, then never returned. Friends came to talk about old times, running through the years quickly, and when there was nothing left to talk about they also disappeared. The only constant had been Frank, who made the six-hour drive every two weeks.

"I've been with Frank for forty-five years now," she said, turning away from the window to look at me. "That's a long time to be with a man."

"He couldn't have been an easy man to live with for some of those years," I said.

"No, his drinking years were difficult. When I left, some of the children told me to never come back."

"Why did you?"

She shrugged.

"I drank myself for a while. I'm not one to pass judgment."

"Did you know Frank was going to quit?"

"I thought he would," she said. "As soon as it slowed him down, I thought he would."

213

I asked about her health and she said a new pre-
scription from the new doctor seemed to be helping.
She didn't have blackouts the way she used to. Didn't
lose track of days as much. I sat there for several
minutes, talking about the weather and being back
in Whitney, before I realized she couldn't remember
my name.

Just then Frank came in and said we had to leave.
The wood was loaded in the bed of the truck and Tom
was waiting. He lived in a trailer next to his dad on
Paradise Road, only a few minutes away.

Frank made a cup of coffee in a steel car mug, then
came over and kissed his wife. The housekeeper had just
walked out of the guest bedroom, looking sheepish at
having slept in.

"Marie, I'll be gone most of the day," he said. "Will
you be all right?"

"I'll be fine, Frank."

Others in Whitney awoke that morning just as startled
by the day.

Walter Sawyer awoke clutching his chest, waiting for
the last mental shards of a bad dream to disappear;
then he rolled out of bed, walked to a window and drew
open the curtains. The sun hit him with the force of a
shower jet.

He stood there a long time, then he drew open
every curtain, opened the front door and sat on a

couch while a pot of coffee brewed, trying to shake the dream. It was a bad heart that had killed his father, a bear of a man who could out-fish, out-hunt and out-fight any man in the highlands. It was a bad heart that had killed his brother Durland, and not a day had passed since when he didn't miss his brother. It was a bad heart that took his only sister as well, Joy dying on the pavement in front of a movie theatre in Oshawa, a long, long time ago.

Arthur had died differently, it was true, but Arthur had always been different. He was a sickly boy, who enjoyed school, never guided, and no one could ever remember when he didn't suffer from epileptic seizures, the familiarity of those attacks perhaps being his undoing. His wife thought nothing of it when he had an attack in the middle of the night—Arthur himself likely thought nothing of it—no surprise at all until the morning, when his wife found his body, curled into a ball, at the end of their bed.

No, it would be his heart that took him, Walter was convinced of that. He had his first heart operation in 1968, was diagnosed with angina in 1974, and on most days he walked around surprised he was still alive. So for the longest time Walter Sawyer sat in the early morning light, thinking of death and wondering where this impossibly beautiful day had come from.

That same morning Gordon Palbiski walked into his kitchen on Hay Lake to find the room bathed in a light that reminded him of a cathedral during mass, a soft glow that stopped him in his tracks and confused him, after nine days of snow, until he realized it was the morning sun reflecting off the frozen lake.

Edmund Kuiack, driving in dawn to his shift at the mill, looked at the fields of snow and thought of a sea, frothy and white, rolling toward some unfamiliar shore, strange stars disappearing one by one as the sun cleared the treeline on Galeairy Lake. He walked into the chipper room with a weariness that surprised him.

Not far away, in the Twin-E and the Parkland restaurant, people talked about the storm and wondered how many feet of snow were in the bush. Some thought four feet. Others argued five. A couple of tree markers having breakfast at the Algonquin Lunchbar across the highway, working for McRae and staying at the East Gate, told the men at the counter they had been at Dickson Lake the week before last and there was already more snow in the bush than they had seen in ten years.

"Don't know how much has fallen since," said one of the tree markers, "but we may be marking the top of the treeline before we're done this year."

People went about their business that morning, working at the mill, buying groceries at the Foodmart, lining up at the Toronto-Dominion, all of them talking about the snow and what a surprise it had been to get out of bed that morning and find the sky a faded blue, the sun visible, the snow so bright you had to shield your eyes to look at it. No one doubted that the storm had passed.

Frank pulled up at Tom's trailer and started to unload the wood, Tom and Neil coming to help. Neil was younger than Walter but looked older. He had to stop every few minutes to catch his breath.

After the wood was stacked we went inside Neil's home and sat on a couch in front of a floor-model colour television. Breakfast dishes sat on nearby television trays. A sewing table stood in a corner. Neil told me he had read the story on Frank and it was nice to see something in the newspaper about fishing. He still enjoyed catching lake trout. Had gone to Opeongo every other day that past summer. Tom took him. Caught so many lake trout he had to "cart them out."

Tom took him and they trolled for lake trout—you can still have a motor on Opeongo, one of the only lakes in the park—and the good spots, he'd known them since he was a boy. Taught them to Tom, the way Basil had taught them to him. So he could probably out-fish Frankie, if he could get around a bit better. Tom's a good boy, he brings him out.

We finished our coffee, then drove around Whitney while I took photos with a disposable camera purchased at the Foodmart. I wanted the photos to remind me of how things looked. The fatigue-green colour of the

McRae Lumber Company sawmill. The Avery Brothers Snowshoes company, the kilns burning and smoke rising through the pines. The Parkland restaurant. The Anglican church. The way the Madawaska River looked running over the dam at Galeairy Lake on a cold, winter's day.

After that we drove to the Algonquin Lunchbar, ordering cheeseburgers and Cokes and sitting at the counter because the lunchroom was filled with snowmobilers. They travelled in packs, loud young men who dressed in black snowsuits emblazoned with corporate logos. Frank had a snowmobile at home, but the track had busted two years ago and he had yet to fix it. Didn't really miss it. Looking around the Lunchbar, he missed it even less.

"So you have some work to do this afternoon?" he asked.

"A few phone calls. I may drop in to see Walter too. What time should we leave?"

We were going ice fishing that night.

"Around four. That'll get us there just before the sun goes down. That's when the ling will start feeding."

"Freshwater cod, right? That's what ling are."

"Right on."

I stared out the window as we ate and saw a line of snowmobilers stretching almost to the highway, waiting to buy gas. The peace of the morning had vanished. There was heavy traffic now on the snowmobile trail that ran through Whitney—the railbed of the old Ottawa, Arnprior and Parry Sound Railway—and on the highway, where lumber trucks were running almost in a convoy, taking advantage of the day to bring out logs from Algonquin park. People walked into the lunchbar for lunch, or to buy a newspaper, and talked to those sitting at the counter as if they had not seen their neighbours in months. People made plans for the weekend.

We finished our cheeseburgers, paid the bill and Frank drove me to the East Gate Motel, saying he would return at four.

Edmund Kuiack finished his shift at the sawmill and returned home, where he sat before a window in the light of mid-afternoon and thought of his wife, who had died the year before. Lorraine had been the strong one, the one who never drank and kept everything together, and there was no logic in her going before Edmund. He wondered if coins were being tossed somewhere.

Gordon Palbiski used a snowblower to clean the driveways and walkways around his home on Hay Lake, shovelled off his roof, then went to bed for an afternoon nap. He dreamed of flying over Algonquin park, in the Cub plane he'd bought in 1965, after getting his pilot's licence. He flew for nearly a decade before a doctor in Pembroke said he couldn't sign the medical clearance, on account of Gordon's heart, no matter how much he yelled. A day like today, with a clear sky and twenty-six inches of ice on some lakes, it would have been grand.

Frankie Van Ball at the Shell station kept pumping gas for the snowmobilers lined up to the highway. Marie read a book. David Kaye looked at the reservation book at the East Gate. The motel would be filled again that night: tree markers, hydro workers, snowmobilers, cross-country skiers, salespeople, long-distance travellers—the ones who travel light, with pillows in the back seat and carry-on luggage in the trunk.

I walked to Walter Sawyer's house, shielding my eyes from the sun, and knocked on his door. He answered, dressed in jeans, a T-shirt and a ball cap that said *Women Love Me, Fish Fear Me.* We sat at his small kitchen table and I asked to see the photo of his father one more time. I stared at the young man in the ten-gallon Stetson, sports jacket and work pants, standing on the shores of Opeongo Lake, holding a lake trout.

"I love this photo," I said, and Sawyer nodded.

"That's the way I remember my dad. Standing by the shore of a lake with a trout in his hand."

"Why is he wearing a sports jacket?"

"Probably got it from some Sport. Probably had a tear in it or something and the guy gave it away. Dad would have been glad to get it."

"Does anyone still pick princess pine?"

"Nah," said Sawyer. "We tried to keep it going for a

Photo by Julie Oliver

Walter Sawyer at his home in Whitney

few years, but it was never the same after Dad died. The company in Toronto makes them out of plastic now."

Frank picked me up at four and we headed west on Highway 60. His ice hut was on Lake of Bays, the other side of Algonquin park. As we drove through the park, Frank pointed out moose tracks in the snow, and a crow's nest, and the spot beside the highway where he'd seen a wolf in a late-August dawn, the morning after a public wolf howl in the park had brought out eight hundred tourists but no wolves were heard. Frank swore the animal was smiling.

We passed Pog Lake campground and then Mew Lake, where campfires could be seen through the spruce and balsam trees; Killarney Lodge, and the turnoff to Bartlett's lodge, both closed in winter; Canoe Lake, where Tom Thomson had drowned more than eighty years earlier; then out the west gate of the park.

We drove through the village of Dwight and down a county road where a road crew had us stuck behind a grader for nearly fifteen minutes, then around a corner and we saw Lake of Bays for the first time. Twenty-three ice huts were set up on the lake, lanterns already turned on in a few. High in the sky I spotted the first clouds of the day.

We parked the truck on a wide stretch of road with other vehicles and started to unload. Frank backed his all-terrain vehicle down a metal ramp from the truck bed, took out his auger, a cooler, some tip-ups and small ice-fishing rods, and loaded everything—including me—onto a sled he hooked up to the ATV. We headed down a path cut through hemlock and birch. When we came through out on the lake the sky had prematurely darkened, the clouds larger now and travelling low. By the time we reached Frank's hut the first flakes were falling.

Frank's hut was the farthest from shore. He had made the hut from a truck cab he had extended with

Photo by Julie Oliver

sheets of plywood so it was tall enough for a man to move around. Inside the hut were a two-burner propane stove, a lantern, a wooden bench and two fold-out metal chairs in front of two holes cut in the ice. Frank removed the wooden boards covering the holes and baited two Williams Wablers with smelt. He dropped the fishing line through the holes, until the lures touched bottom, and then reeled up a foot. He kept one rod in his hand, handed the other to me and chubbed the hole by throwing in more smelt. They spun and twirled as they sank in the water, small, silver fish that took a long time to disappear.

The water in the holes was a shimmering light green

Photo by Julie Oliver

on the surface, but darkened quickly. On some lakes the water was so clear Frank said holes in the ice let you see right to the bottom, where fish would pass slowly over the rocks and sand.

As he jigged the rod Frank stood up and looked out one of the rectangular windows of the hut. The wind had picked up, kicking up the snow that had fallen on the frozen lake in great white swells. There was an island not far from the hut, the shore lined with tall spruce and what looked to be a small clump of white pine, and when the snow rose from the lake the island was briefly lost from sight, only to reappear when the wind eased. It was like looking at a ghost ship.

Frank handed me his rod, then lit the propane stove and put on a pot of water for coffee. It was strange that a storm would come at the end of a day like this, but somewhere there was a logic to it—you just weren't allowed to know what it was. Like the fact a drowned man will surface on the eighth day, who can explain that? But it had happened too many times to be a coincidence. The painter Tom Thomson, they say it happened to him. And Frank's brother, Ambrose, after he drowned on a log run on the Petawawa, jumping from log to log, only one more to go when he was swept under the boom. His best friend, Oscar Dechenes, had searched the river long after everyone else had stopped and, sure enough, he found Ambrose's body on the eighth day, being rocked gently on the waves in a small river bay.

He missed Ambrose. He didn't know anyone who had lived as long as he had and not lost a brother or a sister, so everyone had to deal with it; but it seemed to get harder as the years went by, not easier, and that was another thing that seemed to make no sense. The most difficult years, it seemed, were always ahead.

Frank made the coffee and returned to his seat. He took back his fishing rod, began jigging and before long had his first ling on the line. He pulled the fish to the surface, then through the hole, the whisker-faced fish flopping on the ice until Frank hit it on the snout with his wooden mallet and threw the fish into a plastic pail. Ling might be the ugliest fish Frank knew of, although if you fillet them properly, cutting the flesh from the spine in long, fat strips, there was probably no fish that tasted better. In the next hour we caught six more ling, pulling their squirming, slender bodies from the dark water, Frank killing them with a wooden mallet by the light of the lantern.

We kept the propane stove going because it was cold outside, the wind buffeting the ice hut, the visibility sometimes no more than a few feet. An hour ago a fishing party in a nearby hut had packed up and left and we were the last ones left on the lake. Pulling ling from the water below, watching the smelts twirl and glisten in the black water, slowly fizzling from view like shooting stars, we lost track of time.

Algonquin Highlands in winter

If you had walked into the hut later that night you would have seen an old man, hunched in a chair, fishing rod in hand, and a younger man sitting beside him. The lantern would have gone out and the only light would have come from the aquamarine water showing through two holes cut in the ice—an eerie, greenish glow that cast moving shadows on the walls of the hut.

The old man would be smoking a cigarette and drinking coffee, the rod in his right hand jerking up and falling every few seconds, as rhythmic as breathing. Outside, a snowstorm would be gathering strength, the biggest storm of the year it would turn out to be, closing highways and schools throughout the Algonquin

Courtesy of Algonquin Park Museum

Highlands by morning. On the frozen lake the snow would swirl and rise in a great white wall, then fall and rise again. On the shoreline of a nearby island, through the snow and the wind, shadows could be seen moving through the trees, as if people were out there. If the old man stood up he might have seen in those shadows the faces of people he once knew: Ambrose; Basil Sawyer;

Jim Holly; Bill Currie; a German couple he saw drown on Opeongo when they didn't head to shore quickly enough with a storm coming, as he stood helpless at the far end of the lake.

If you stayed in the hut for any length of time you would have seen both men catch fish—the sharp jerk of the rod, the line reeled in, a ling pulled from the green water, the old man hitting the fish with a wooden mallet, then throwing the still-twitching body into a plastic pail. Near midnight, you would have seen something different, although it would start the same way—a jerk of the rod, the line reeled in—but no whiskers this time on the fish that burst through the water. The old man would have raised his mallet, then hesitated, looking at the silver colouring of the fish, the distinctive V-shaped fin. If you strained to hear through the wind and the snow slashing the hut, you might have heard the old man say, "Gawd, that's a nice fish."

And then you would have seen him cradle the fish gently in his hands, before letting it slide through his fingers, headfirst, back into the water.

"Next year," you would have heard him say, although you would soon wonder if he'd actually said it, or if it was the wind you heard—one of those whispers when the wind passes through the trees, or kicks up snow on a frozen lake.

"Next year."

Shortly after midnight Frank reeled in his lure, loaded the ATV with the catch, and we set off across the lake, stopping several times to rock the vehicle when it got stuck in the snow. As we looked at the snow falling through a starless sky, we knew we had stayed too long and Marie would be waiting. We had to hurry.

And did you get what
You wanted from this life, even so?
I did.
And what did you want?
To call myself beloved, to feel myself
Beloved on the earth.

Raymond Carver

Acknowledgements

Several editors at the *Ottawa Citizen* have to be thanked for backing this story from the day I met Frank Kuiack. Without the support and encouragement of *Citizen* Editor-in-Chief Scott Anderson, Managing Editor Lynn McAuley (who first assigned the story), Managing Editor Don Butler, and weekly magazine Editor Susan Allan, this book would not have been possible.

Citizen photographer Julie Oliver, originally from Belfast, who caught her first trout on Ragged Lake, took most of the photos in the book and cannot be thanked enough. She takes a lovely photo, "So she does."

Barbara Berson, senior editor at Penguin Books Canada, commissioned this book after receiving an e-mail and a newspaper clipping. I must also thank Cynthia Good and Janet Dea of Penguin, and editor Charis Wahl.

Researching this book needed the help of many

people at Algonquin park: Chief Naturalist Rick Stronks, former Chief Naturalist Dan Strickland, Mike Runtz and Archivist Charlotte Woodley all gave freely of their time and expertise. Eugene and Helen Katz of Arowhon Pines provided a pleasant base for the initial research.

There are almost too many people in Whitney to thank, although Bernie Stubbs Jr., Walter and Neil Sawyer, Frankie Van Ball, Catherine Van Ball, Gordon and Clover Palbiski, Mike and Danny Avery and Edmund Kuiack come easily to mind.

Numerous friends and family members need to be thanked, for acts of kindness as significant as reading a rough manuscript, to simply saying the right thing on the right day: John Owens, Roy MacGregor, Jed Rached, Gary Thaine, Nancy Besserer, RayDawn Weinstein, Pat Hyndman, Connie Defalco, Dave Wilson, John Morrissy, Scott Sigurdson, Pat and Terry McGregor, Bernadette Corbett, and Christina and Graham Greig. I should also thank Bob Dylan for writing "Things Have Changed," which helped many nights more than any exhortation from an editor.

Lastly, I would like to thank my father, Robert James Corbett, for first taking me fishing in Algonquin park.